D0548311

WITHDRAWN
FROM STOCK

Live While You Can

Fr. Tony Coote was Parish Priest in the parish of Mount Merrion and Kilmacud in Dublin, Ireland, from 2008 until his death on 28 August 2019. In July 2018, just months after being diagnosed with motor neurone disease, Tony organised and took part in Walk While You Can, a fundraising walk from Letterkenny, County Donegal to Ballydehob, County Cork to raise money and awareness of the disease. The walk of over 550 kilometres received national attention with Tony completing the journey in his wheelchair. In December 2018, Tony was awarded an Honorary Doctorate from UCD for outstanding service to the community recognising the role he played with the now nationwide student-led mental health movement 'Please Talk', and for his work in setting up UCD Volunteer Overseas.

Fr Tony Coote left behind him a legacy of friendship and love.

Live While You Can

A Memoir of Faith, Hope and the Power of Acceptance

FR. TONY COOTE

HACHETTE
BOOKS
IRELAND

Leabharlann
Contae na Mídhe

*I dedicate this book to
those I love and all those who live with
motor neurone disease all over the world.
One day there will be a cure.*

First published in 2019 by Hachette Books Ireland

This edition first published in 2020

Copyright © Fr. Tony Coote, 2019

Excerpt from *The Crucified God* by Jürgen Moltmann © 1973.
Reprinted by permission of Fortress Press.

Excerpt from *God, Where Are You?* by Enzo Bianchi.
Reproduced with permission of The Licensor through PLSclear.

The Seven Story Mountain by Thomas Merton.
Reproduced with permission of The Licensor through PLSclear.

The author and publisher have made every effort to contact all copyright holders.
We apologise for any omissions or errors and will endeavour to rectify this
at the earliest opportunity.

All rights reserved. No part of this publication may be reproduced, stored in a
retrieval system, or transmitted, in any form or by any means without the prior
written permission of the publisher, nor be otherwise circulated in any form of binding
or cover other than that in which it is published and without a similar condition
being imposed on the subsequent purchaser.

A CIP catalogue record for this title is available from the British Library

ISBN: 9781529396287

Book design and typesetting: Anú Design, Tara
Boat image © Paul Grand/Trevillion Images
Printed and bound by Clays Ltd, Elcograf, S.p.A

Hachette Books Ireland policy is to use papers that are natural,
renewable and recyclable products and made from wood grown in
sustainable forests. The logging and manufacturing processes are expected to
conform to the environmental regulations of the country of origin.

Hachette Books Ireland
8 Castlecourt Centre
Castleknock
Dublin 15, Ireland

A division of Hachette UK Ltd
Carmelite House
50 Victoria Embankment
London EC4Y 0DZ

www.hachettebooksireland.ie

Contents

Acknowledgements

I want to thank Adam Gaine for his patience and time in typing all the text. We laughed and cried for many months piecing it together. The book would never have happened without the enthusiasm and support of Roisín Gallagher and Emily Hourican. I also thank Breda Purdue and Ciara Doorley from Hachette for seeing the potential of this book and being prepared to bring it to a wider public.

I express my gratitude to the Archbishop of Dublin, Diarmuid Martin, and all my colleagues in the priesthood, especially those I have ministered with over the years.

I thank all those I served in Ballymun, UCD, Mount Merrion and Kilmacud from whom I've learned so much that benefited my life.

Friends are so important in every aspect of life, so I thank all those who have been a friend to me and shown me the true value of friendship.

My family have supported me all the way through my life, especially in my priesthood, so with love I thank my brothers David, Kieran and Pat. And my nieces and nephews Tom, Lily, Jasmyn, Khloe, Charlie, Tara, Rían, Eve, Oscar and Mikey.

Finally, the hero of our family is our mother Patricia. We all love her dearly, and everything we have has come about through her resilience and care.

Fr Tony Coote, January 2019

Foreword

Noise is a big part of all our lives, but for me it's almost a constant companion. In work, it's the frantic communication of deadlines and ideas and getting shows to air. In life, it's the radio – almost always current affairs – or the phone or the internet, trying not to miss anything that's happening in the world. Or it's the children and the radio and the dog and the relentless whirr of the washing machine and the noise of the to-do list in my head churning the things that didn't get done again today.

There is one moment in my week, however, which is almost always calm. On Monday nights, after the credits have rolled on the television show I present, *Claire Byrne Live*, I get into my car at about 12.30 a.m. for the twenty-minute drive home. Usually, the radio comes on in the car and at that time it's a music show and for once I don't fumble to switch to find a talk station; instead, I allow myself to really enjoy the music and to take a few deep breaths and relax.

On Monday, 24 September 2018 I sat into the car after the show and when the radio came on I tried to follow my routine and enjoy the song that was playing, but my head felt crowded and so I switched it off and drove in silence. My brain insisted on this in order to process what had happened that night and the profound impact it had on me.

That was the night I met Father Tony Coote. He was on the show to tell us about his Walk While You Can initiative. I had read and heard about Father Coote's mission the previous summer to get from the top of Ireland to the bottom, and it was clear that he was a force to be reckoned with. I'm sure most would agree that, faced with the devastating news that they have a condition like motor neurone disease, a physically challenging awareness campaign would not be top of the to-do list. So part of me expected to meet a unique person, but I wasn't prepared for the force of nature who won me over, and indeed the rest of the country, that night.

We had a brief chat before the interview and the first thing I noticed was the joy around him and the sparkle in his eyes and the good humour. Good humour follows this man in spades and his optimism and pragmatism is infectious. It was that pragmatism and the 'let's just get on with it' spirit that stopped me in my tracks. There I was, feeling tired after a long day, worried about minor troubles, allowing little things to bother me, and I was talking to this person who can no longer walk or lift his hands and whose future is inescapably bleak. Meeting Tony Coote is the kick in the behind that many of us need.

After his appearance on the show, I stayed in touch with Tony, and a few months later I attended his special conferring ceremony at UCD where he was awarded a doctorate. It was a wonderful occasion, and Professor Joe Carthy, Dean of Science, jokingly said that Tony has been claimed by so many people – from parishioners, to friends, colleagues at UCD, and so many others who have crossed his path and feel that he is somehow 'theirs' – it is hard to know whom he belongs to. But once you meet him, you understand utterly why that is so.

Since I met Doctor Coote, who tells me that this is how I should now address him (!), I have heard many stories from others about the quiet ways he has helped individuals throughout his life: about his compassion, lack of judgement and unshakeable belief that everyone who needs support and help should get it, regardless of what they may have done in the past or the perceived hopelessness of their situation. I know also that he has begun national movements relating to mental health and volunteering overseas that have started as an idea in his head and – due in no small part, no doubt, to his stubborn nature – have grown to affect positively so many people in this country and far beyond.

Tony freely admits that he does not like his illness and some days he hates what it is doing to him, but he refuses to waste his energy hating the fact that he has MND. Hating it isn't going to stop its progression and it's not going to do him any good. Instead, he uses his time to campaign for help for those who are coming after him – to raise funds for research – and for nursing care for those with the disease now. He has also written this book, in part to tell us how he has lived his life, how he has tried to stay true to his three pillars – inclusivity, compassion and love.

It is hard to see any good in what has happened to Tony Coote, but would he have written this book if MND had not come along? Would the whole of Ireland have come to know this remarkable person and been touched by his outlook on life had he not been struck by MND? From my own perspective, I may never have met him had it not been for his diagnosis and subsequent campaign. I know that my life is richer as a result and I'm sure, when you turn the last page of this book, yours will be too.

I am honoured to introduce this book to you for my friend, Father (Doctor) Tony Coote.

Claire Byrne, 2019

Prologue

As I write this, it is New Year's Day 2019.

Exactly one year ago, at the age of fifty-three, in the same room where I am now, I had a fall that began a massive change in my life.

It led to a diagnosis of motor neurone disease, and the rapid loss of muscle tone, ability and my independence.

When I look back, it's like looking at a different world.

Like many people, I look both backwards and forwards. I don't know exactly what the future will bring, although I know I will probably not be alive this time next year. But this doesn't scare me at all.

I have never been afraid of death. I know it frightens some people to hear me talk like this, but it is what I truly feel. The future still holds promise and I know I will continue to live every day to the fullest. I have always said that I'll do what I can, as long as I can. And when I can't, I can't.

Even though my time is short, I'm not in any rush to do things I have never done before or to see places I have never seen before.

Each day, I savour memories of the past. Many of these make me laugh and some make me cry. If I cry, it's because I see the faces of those I love and I am conscious of the fact that soon I will be saying goodbye. It is probably true that all memories contain both laughter and tears.

But there is no morbid atmosphere in my home. Rather, it is a place filled with activity, with comings and goings, storytelling and the emptying of many bottles with a '%' sign on the label.

I want to write the story of my life, and tell the story of my faith, while I still can. I want to write with honesty and compassion, for myself and others. I want also to recognise that in all our lives there is pain and loss and difficulty. But there is help too, and answers.

Wednesday, 28 February 2018

I woke in my house in Mount Merrion, Dublin around 6.30 a.m. I hadn't had much sleep. I had an appointment that morning in the Beacon hospital. I went to the window; the whole area was covered in snow. Normally on a Wednesday I would have had my parish duties to attend to, but that day the entire country was at a standstill owing to the heaviest fall of snow in years.

At around eight I phoned the hospital to say I was postponing because of the weather. However, when I looked out again an hour later, I saw cars making their way up the road, so I decided I would head to the Beacon after all. My appointment was with a neurologist for 10.30 and we were to discuss the results of a brain scan I'd had about ten days earlier.

The reason for the scan was because I'd had two falls. The first was in early November when I was coming down the steps of the Church of Saint Thérèse in Mount Merrion. I was carrying a box and suddenly, without explanation, I fell, hitting my shoulder off a wall and my knee on the ground. An elderly man who was passing helped to pick me up. 'Offer it up, Father,' he said. I was convinced I was rushing, as usual, and had just missed a step.

Then on New Year's Day various members of my family were visiting for lunch. Just before dessert, I went in to the sitting room to put some logs on the fire and I suddenly fell face down on the floor, again for no apparent reason. Everyone came running and I heard someone say, 'He's had a stroke.' Gently, they tried to lift me and were encouraging me to use my left hand to raise myself up. I told them I had no power in that hand, which seemed to confirm their suspicions about a stroke. Eventually they got me onto a chair and advised me to go to a hospital or call a doctor. I protested that I just needed some time because I was in a state of shock.

My guests started to leave, but only after making sure I had water and was okay to stand up. Over the next few days, my brother Pat stayed in touch to remind me to make an appointment with a doctor. I had only seen a doctor three times in my adult life, all in relation to issues with my elbow from playing squash.

It took me two days to call a GP, who prescribed anti-inflammatory pain relief and advised me to take two weeks off – which I spent in Glendalough – to allow my knee and leg to heal because I still had pain there. During this time, I noticed that my knee wasn't particularly swollen, and yet I still had pain there, and also in my shoulder. I asked my GP to arrange for me to have scans of both. The results showed nothing sinister, just the expected tissue damage, so she referred me to an orthopaedic consultant in the Beacon and also a neurologist.

A week later I met the orthopaedic consultant, who had reviewed my scans, and he said that there was nothing there that he could detect. He asked me to describe any particular symptoms I was experiencing, and I said that sometimes my leg went into an involuntary spasm and began to shake. He said this was known as clonus, and I read something in his face that suggested it might be serious. He asked if I intended to see a neurologist and I told him I had an appointment for later that week.

The neurologist said that some of my symptoms were consistent with a stroke, but she couldn't detect anything definite and so arranged for a brain scan. Those were the results I was waiting for on that February day.

And so it was that on that snowy morning in February I was heading to the Beacon Hospital. And yet there was a nagging feeling within me that said if it had been a stroke, I would have been called back sooner. Perhaps that was why I hadn't slept much during the night.

The hospital was mainly deserted except for a few staff who had braved the weather. My neurologist took me into a small bay behind a curtain and began to give me the results of my brain scan. She said that a radiographer and consultant radiographer had initially seen nothing in the scan but when she looked again she saw what she called scrapings, which told her I had motor neurone disease (MND).

She asked if I had considered that possibility. I said I hadn't, that I had resisted researching my symptoms online to find out more. At the time I knew very little about MND.

I know far more now, of course. Motor neurone diseases are a group of neurodegenerative disorders that selectively affect motor neurons, the cells which control voluntary muscles of the body. Each motor neurone disease affects patients differently, but they all cause movement-related symptoms, mainly muscle weakness. The rate of progression can be very different: some patients will be relatively symptom-free for years, while others will have a much faster onset.

I can't say what was going through my mind at that moment when the neurologist first mentioned MND, but on reflection I suspect that my body was going into shock. She asked me to undress because she was going to carry out some tests that I later learned were called electromyography (EMG), and a nerve conduction test that involved sticking needles into my muscles and applying electroshock to my feet, which would give her readings on a laptop. The readings were not clear, so the consultant had to twist the needle deeper into my muscles.

I have thought about this many times since: what a cruel test for such a cruel illness – sticking needles into muscles, inflicting pain when so much pain would be on the way.

The tests took well over an hour, after which time the consultant said that there was one more place where she had to put the needle – in my tongue. 'No way,' I said. 'I'm not having that.'

'I understand,' she replied sympathetically. 'You've had enough for one day.'

She left me to get dressed. However, there was a lot of gel still on my hands and arms that had been applied before the tests, so I went to the sink to wash it off. Turning around to put my clothes back on, I fell flat onto the floor. This wasn't quite like previous falls. I think it was shock this time that raced through my body and flung me down.

The consultant came back in. 'Oh you poor man,' she said.

I left the hospital and drove home through empty streets as the snow continued to fall. Everywhere was white and still and unfamiliar, outlines changed by the blanket of snow and the whirling flakes. Consequently the journey took longer than usual and my mind was full of thoughts about what would happen to me, who I would tell and how. Reaching home, I went straight into the sitting room, still in my coat, the ticking of the clock the only sound I heard. For some time I just stared out the window. Each house was almost hidden behind thick drifts of snow. I watched the world outside and it was peaceful, with hardly a car passing or a person walking by. I stood there for some time. I suppose I was letting the news I'd received seep into me and land there, amid feelings of confusion, fear and terror.

Later that day I contacted my brothers – Pat, Kieran and David – to tell them the news. Pat and Kieran both live in Dublin, while David is in Australia. There was, I think, a mixture of shock and confusion when they heard. Like so many people, they didn't understand the full weight of my diagnosis. Pat, the youngest, who lives in Ballinteer, wanted to come over, but by then the snow was much heavier and I asked him not to. It wasn't safe to drive, and it was quite a journey on foot.

I then phoned the Archbishop of Dublin, Diarmuid Martin, to tell him my news. That summer, I was due to move from the parishes of Mount Merrion and Kilmacud, where I had served for nearly ten years, and I asked him if I could remain in the post since I knew so many people there. I feared that by taking up a new appointment, I would arrive in a new place, a stranger, and would inevitably be known as 'the sick priest'. To my relief, the archbishop agreed and assured me that he and the diocese would help me in any way they could.

After making my calls, and when one of the neighbours had supplied me with fire-lighters, I settled down in front of the blazing fire with a glass of rich red wine.

I went to bed late and didn't sleep. My mind was spinning, thinking about how the diagnosis would affect my life. I could hear the wind outside blowing harder and bringing more snow, and I tossed and turned, probably for most of that night. Of course, the night has a tendency to magnify everything. In its stillness you know – and I surely knew that night – that you are alone.

Thursday, 1 March 2018

The next morning, the road outside was completely covered with snow. My house has a large front room which looks onto the street, beside the church carpark. Beside the church is the local national school, and so from my front room I can hear children and their parents walking up and down, to and from school, several times a day. The house is always busy – friends and parishioners drop in frequently. At the back is a peaceful garden.

On this day, though, owing to the weather, the street was completely deserted. On the path up to my door the snow was perhaps three feet deep and so I didn't feel I could venture out safely. But I suppose too that I didn't want to meet people in a half-cheery way while inside I was still in turmoil, trying to figure out what the hell was going on. I phoned some of my parishioners and told them the news, and they arrived with food and other supplies to help me through the next few days. One of them brought a bunch of daffodils that had not yet flowered and placed them in a glass on my coffee table. Some were crying and I did my best to console them. This is so often the case when we break dreadful news to people – the person with the illness becomes the consoler to those they tell.

I accepted their kindness gratefully but inside I was terrified. I've always been an independent person and have felt responsible in some way for those around me, something that had been instilled in me, no doubt, from childhood.

*

I suppose being the eldest child, and given the circumstances of our upbringing, I have always had a strong sense of responsibility for my brothers and my mother. I was born on 16 June 1964 in Holles Street hospital to Patricia Rigney from Fairview and Patrick Coote from Ennis in County Clare. I grew up in Fairview in Dublin. My mother worked in a solicitor's office on the quays until she married and, as was the law in Ireland at the time, had to give up her job. My father had been in the Irish Army as part of the UN peacekeeping missions to the Congo, but by the time I was born he had left the armed forces and was training to be a physical education teacher. My parents went on to have four more boys: David, born a year after me, then Kieran three years later, followed by Alan, who died when he was very young, and then Pat.

My mother and father married in 1963 after meeting at the Metropole Dance Hall in Dublin. My mother's sister Pauline, who was unmarried, lived with us in Fairview. Ours was a happy childhood, with many good memories and lots of friends. I remember long summers playing Subbuteo in each other's homes or else being out all day. We had much more freedom then than many children have now, out all day until 'tea time'.

I wasn't much good at football, but I used to take on the role of referee if we organised teams to play in the park. My main passion was running, though, and every Monday evening, as part of a local athletics club, I would run from Fairview out along the coast road, through Clontarf to Dollymount Strand and back.

On Sundays, as a family, we would go for what was known as a Sunday drive. We typically headed towards the Sugar Loaf mountain in Wicklow or on towards Wexford.

Fairview Green was also the home place of my mother and her family. Her parents had bought the house where we lived in early 1927. As a child, I remember some neighbours who had known my grandmother, who died in 1963, before I was born. Several times a month I would shop for some of these elderly neighbours, particularly Mrs O'Neill, for whom I would buy groceries and untipped cigarettes, and Mr Dunne, who would give me his shopping trolley and I would go with my list to Angela Leavy's store on Fairview Strand. Angela knew everyone and so when I handed in the list, she knew exactly what Mr Dunne was looking for. Once a week, we would do our own shopping and all walk to the Howth Road to the H. Williams supermarket. My mother now had a little troupe of helpers, willing and unwilling, to carry the messages home.

It was a wonderful community to grow up in, with these wise, elderly neighbours. I remember another lady we knew as Granny Coyne, with false teeth that used to chatter and who used to dribble on her chin, which she would wipe away with a little lace handkerchief. One day she said to me, 'Always remember, faith moves mountains!' I laughed and asked, 'How can you move a mountain?' but Granny Coyne had great faith and ignored my question.

In 1972 our small household was to face its first devastating loss shortly after Alan, the second youngest, was born. Like she'd done previously, my mother went into the Rotunda for the birth. Mam returned home some days later with Alan but from the outset I knew that this wasn't like it had been with Kieran. Sadly, Alan was born with leukemia and was very sick from birth. I remember being at his baptism in Crumlin hospital in May 1972. At that stage I didn't fully understand how sick he was.

A month later, it was my eighth birthday, which I share with a cousin, and as children we used to have a joint party. At the party, we were all out in the back garden playing and in the middle of a game, I remember a little girl saying to me, 'Your baby is dead.' I ran inside looking for my mother and saw people standing around her. That was my first experience of grief and I didn't fully understand it at the time, although I could tell by looking at my mother's face that something terrible had happened. Looking back, I know that what I saw on her face was heartbreak.

The following week, my father went to collect Alan's coffin and then came back to collect my mother. I saw the little white coffin in the car, but I never saw Alan. I remember my parents leaving for the burial. I begged to go, but they wouldn't let me. I remember my father's Renault 16 disappearing around the corner, and that I stayed all day looking out that window until they came home. I felt anger that they wouldn't bring me. I had been at Alan's baptism just a month before, but they wouldn't let me go to the funeral. And I remember, clearly, that I wanted Alan back.

I expected my parents to have Alan with them when they came back, but they had nothing. As a child, you don't understand death. You understand people leaving – but you expect them to come back.

My Aunt Pauline came in several times to ask me to come away from the window, but I wouldn't. When my parents finally came home, my mother went straight up the stairs and into her room. My father patted me on the head and said I should get something to eat. Nothing more.

When you're eight, you can't process all those things. You just know what happened. Something inside me that day told me that my parents were not able to help me. I remember thinking to myself, *They can't help me*, and somehow knowing that I would manage. I don't think I used those words, it was just a feeling I had.

One of my earliest memories was being shown a statue of Saint Anthony of Padua, by my paternal grandmother. She told me that the child in his arms was Jesus, so from a very young age I've been aware of the name of Jesus and who he was. As a child, I prayed more to my guardian angel, however, and indeed when Alan died, even though I was very upset when my mother told me that he was a little angel in heaven, I never questioned that. Then we used to pray to Alan to ask God to help us.

Then in the mid-1970s my parents decided to move from Fairview to rent a larger house in Santry. This was a huge upheaval – although we were able to stay in our schools in Fairview – but that house in Santry meant that for the first time I had my own bedroom, something that in those days was a luxury.

Life continued on as we all struggled with Alan's loss in our own ways. We had good neighbours, and because my father was now doing well financially, with his own driving school and a job as a PE teacher, he started socialising more regularly and began to invite these neighbours in for parties. He was quite the man about town in those days, and seemed to be very popular. But all was not well with my parents. Grief for Alan had come between them, but so had my father's drinking.

Often when the parties were over, I would hear my father and mother arguing, and over time, these arguments became more regular. Doors would bang and I'd hear my mother cry. It's funny how as a child you place the covers over your head so you can't hear, believing that in some way, under this little tent of protection, everything will be okay.

My father began to drink more and more. From what I remember, he drank whiskey, and although he wasn't an alcoholic – he could take it or leave it, and certainly wasn't drunk all the time – drink never suited him. He was especially bad having taken whiskey. In fact, it made him crazy. He threw his own parents out of our house one night, after they had come for an evening visit. He was not an easy man to live with, and even less so when drinking.

I try to give him the benefit of the doubt, because of his life. He had been a soldier in the Congo in the late 1950s with the UN, and one of his friends was killed in the Niemba ambush of 1960, in which nine Irish soldiers lost their lives. He never talked about it, although it may have been the reason he left the army, and after he died in 2013 we found his blue beret and his medals from that time in a safety deposit box. In all likelihood there was something going on in his head that he couldn't express.

The sad irony is that when my mother married him,

one of the most important things for her was that he wore a Pioneer pin, showing his commitment to total abstinence from alcohol. Her own father had been an alcoholic, which badly affected her family when she was a child, and so she deliberately chose a man who didn't drink. Not at the time anyway.

I used to think my mother was too good, too quiet, but it's only when you think about it you realise how mental and physical abuse takes its toll over the years. And in those days, no one wanted to hear it. There was no one for her to talk to. Her family had been banned from the house by my father long before, so she couldn't easily talk to them.

The arguments culminated in an event that was the beginning of the end of my parents' marriage. My Uncle Anthony, my father's brother, a priest, was home from South America, and my father took him out for the day and said he would be back at a certain time. My mother had prepared the dinner, but she didn't hear from my father. He and Anthony were very late getting home. My mother had the dinner in the oven to keep it warm, but when she placed it on the table my father shouted that it was burned and pushed the plate off the table. It smashed on the ground. My father shouted at my mother to 'F**k off', saying that he had somebody else and didn't need her.

I witnessed all this. I was very close to my uncle and had wanted to see him, so I was there in the kitchen with them when my father threw the plate.

From that evening, my mother slept in the spare room, which was downstairs, and locked her door every night. I used to hear my father trying to get into that room, banging and banging on the door. The atmosphere in the house began to decline even further. We all cringed when we heard his car pulling into the driveway.

There were times I hated my father. I saw him as a bully and I tried to stand up for my mother. I went down one night – he was banging on the bedroom door – and told him to leave her alone. He ordered me back upstairs, and then he came up after me, into my bedroom, and said, 'Don't ever f**king challenge me again!' I thought he was going to hit me, but he didn't. We were all hit as kids, as was normal then, but there was something different about that night. He was very angry, but he knew I hated him, really hated him, and that this was the end of something, and so he didn't raise his fist.

Soon after that, one of our neighbours who had been a regular guest at the parties in our house said to my mother that my father didn't fool her. She had heard the arguments and knew what he could be like. From that moment, my mother began to believe that she could leave my father. And it turned out that more of the neighbours knew about him than ever let on, so when we needed help, they gave it.

One weekend while my father was at a conference, we just upped and left. Some of the neighbours came to our house and helped us to carry all the furniture to a new house around the corner that my mother had somehow rented, a chain of tables and chairs travelling up the street. That evening, one of the neighbours gave us a casserole for our dinner and many others offered to help in any way they could.

On the Sunday night, we saw our father returning to the house. He must have got a shock when he went inside and saw it was nearly empty. He asked neighbours where we were, but nobody would tell him. He couldn't see us but we could see him from an upstairs window in our new home.

Within a couple of years my parents separated legally, and my father moved to live in Clontarf, so at last we had some freedom.

During the court hearings for the separation, there was discussion about payment of child support for us four boys. My father contested. He even said that my mother was a religious fanatic. When she told me he had said this, I wrote a letter to the judge stating that our mother was kind and was looking after us as best she could. I challenged what my father had said. The judge read the letter out in court and my father asked me to withdraw it. I told him that I couldn't, because what he said about Mam was untrue. I didn't see my father again for over thirty years. I was twelve years old.

People often said to me in the intervening years, 'How come you never saw your father?' And I'd reply, 'We at home were busy living.' And in any case there was very little effort on my father's part for any sustained contact with his children.

With him gone, we had much more freedom and were much happier. We used to sit downstairs in the evenings and laugh – roar with laughter. All my mother's family would come around every week to see how we were.

My mother became a different person when my father left. She was very strong – she had to be, with four children and, at first, no job. But I look back with such admiration at her courage. I watched as she became more assertive and determined, even though she was often socially isolated by other women who would say, for example, if they were all going to a dance, 'Oh, we've no room in the car', or 'We didn't think you'd want to come.' And yet she found friends, she found a life outside our home. She is an amazing woman, the big star of our childhood.

My father gave her a little bit of money for Pat, who was very young, and she got a deserted wives' allowance, and then there were her jobs – she took on two jobs caring for elderly people in their homes to ensure that we had enough to live on. Even so, often there barely was, and I certainly never felt in our family that we had much money, although we were happy.

My father leaving brought other troubles too. It's not easy for boys to be brought up with no father, and we were always fighting one another. Mam was finding it very difficult to manage everyone, especially as we moved into our teenage years. At first, one of my uncles used to come down and threaten us – 'Are you behaving?' – and that was enough. Later, one of my brothers ran away from home. Luckily a local community garda was very kind to my mother, and the few threats he gave to my brother when he came home ensured that this never happened again.

I spent a lot of my childhood feeling responsible for my mother and my siblings – a role that I took on voluntarily as the eldest boy. Like the boy staring out the window at Alan's coffin, I always tried to 'manage' by myself.

The early experiences of any human being are the most lasting; they go much deeper than anything that happens later. At that age, your parents (and sometimes

your teachers) are everything to you. If they vanish, or seem to let you down, you fall back on yourself. There is strength in that, but a loneliness too.

That period of my life was one of great change, and change is never easy. It can be accompanied by destruction of some kind, and maybe loss. But I always had that feeling of being able to manage, whether that was through religious faith even at that young age, or through the necessity of the situation and the responsibility I felt for my mother and siblings.

Looking out the window at the snow after coming home from the Beacon hospital knowing I had MND, I had that same feeling again, that I was going to manage. I've always managed, but in some ways that hinders me as much as it helps me. There is a streak of independence in it. And stubbornness. It can be a trap – you think you can take on the whole world. But no one can take on the whole world on their own.

I had been due to say mass but we made a decision to keep the church closed, mainly to discourage people from trying to get there in the snow as the church is situated at the top of a steep hill. At this stage, children and their

parents were using anything they could find as makeshift toboggans to slide down the church carpark and onto the road, with no fear of encountering a passing car. I could hear the screams of laughter.

I never researched this illness online. I didn't need to, and I didn't see the point – I had been told that MND is different from person to person; another person's experience would not necessarily be mine. Anyway, my body was already dealing with its effects and my illness was increasingly evident even since the first fall. I had begun to drag my left leg behind me when I walked, and I could feel that my left hand was closing gradually, stiffening into a clenched fist. But I needed time to take in the implications.

Had circumstances been different, there would have been many people coming in and out of the house, but the snow meant that could not happen and so I had time to plan how I was going to approach my new situation.

I sat in my sitting room and prayed, as I always have done, in my own simple and inadequate words, asking Jesus to be with me and not abandon me through these days and months.

I don't know how long I spent praying but eventually those sounds of laughter and screams of delight penetrated my consciousness, and stirred in me a strong desire that

I have still not lost – the desire to live, no matter what this illness will bring. I knew then that I was going to live as best I could. Over the next few days, the daffodils a parishioner had brought blossomed, full of colour, and became a symbol of my own awakening and the dawning of a new reality.

Sermon – Easter Vigil

So what we celebrate tonight is the power of transformation, how an apparent tragedy brings salvation, how scared people become brave, how the misery of someone who let down his friend is changed to courage by the forgiveness of that friend and ultimately how death has been defeated for ever because, as Jesus was raised from the dead, we too will travel on that journey.

Tonight also celebrates the impossible being made possible. Where in our lives are we giving up on others, and ourselves, where are we refusing to see hope, or are refusing to forgive? Light has come into our world. Let us all reach out to stand in its glow and bring it from here to others.

Friday, 2 March 2018

On Friday evening, two of my best friends, Liam and Carl, who both live nearby, said they would collect me and bring me to their house for dinner. Carl was unable to drive up my road so he parked on the nearby N11 and I walked down to meet him. Snow was still thick on the ground and many of the smaller roads were impassable. But it was a beautiful night, and the air was clear and cold and there were stars in the black sky.

Someone had loaned me a walking stick with a spike at the end that let me move with a fair degree of balance and I had got up a good speed, prompting Carl to say when he saw me that he didn't think it could be me as I was going so fast.

Liam had cooked a lovely meal. We had some wine, a good chat, and I stayed the night in their place and had the best sleep I'd had in a few days. During the meal both Carl and Liam were encouraging and very positive. They were tapping into my own belief at this stage that my motor neurone disease was fairly benign – as it can be, with some patients feeling relatively few effects for quite some time – and so believing that I could manage as I was for perhaps a number of years.

After breakfast Liam dropped me back to my house. The snow had begun to slowly thaw. Liam got a shovel and cleared my path. All around the area people were doing something similar. Others were out shopping, even though the local supermarket was quickly running out of stock, and more cars were venturing out.

Sunday, 4 March 2018

On Sunday morning I was due to say mass in the Church of Saint Thérèse beside my house. I woke early to the sounds of shovels scraping the ground. I got dressed and went outside and saw a group of local parishioners clearing a pathway through the church carpark to help those who would be coming to mass.

I went out to thank them. They had been marshalled

by one of our parish secretaries, Maggie, who had sent out a message appealing to as many people as possible to help clear the church carpark. By late morning, that number of volunteers had grown steadily and they had done a tremendous job.

I celebrated mass, and said nothing of my illness because, although news was slowly getting out, I needed time before announcing it to the whole parish. After mass, my brother Pat came to the church to collect me and walk me down through the carpark. I was delighted to see him as I had been a bit afraid that I would slip. Even since the Tuesday, it felt like the drag of my left leg had become more prominent, and together with the closing of my left hand, this left me unsteady, particularly in the snow.

I had arranged to meet my family in Gleesons pub on Booterstown Avenue for lunch. Pat would drive me down. This was to be my first time seeing them all since receiving my news. My mother had been diagnosed with Alzheimer's around the same time. The only slight bit of comfort in this is that I knew the full weight of my diagnosis would not be clear to her, and although she did express sadness, her emotional response was more muted than it would otherwise have been. I thought to myself, *At least Mam won't really know how sick I am.* I've always been close to my mother. My earliest memory is from 1968, when I was four. She had gone into hospital as there had been complications with her pregnancy with Kieran. Myself and David had been left at home in the care of Aunt Pauline but Mam was gone for four days and it was the longest she had ever been away from us and we were terrified. I suppose I just missed her.

The lunch was a fun-filled occasion. I realised very early on that, when dealing with a diagnosis like this, your family very much take the lead from you in how to approach it. And so my positive outlook rubbed off on them and there was never going to be a 'poor-me' attitude.

So lunch was not celebrated under a pall of gloom, but rather with our usual back and forth slagging and discussing plans we all had for the rest of the year. My mother smiled through it all in an almost surreal fashion. She was content and therefore I was too – still believing that I could manage this diagnosis and continue as I was for many years.

The parish had long planned a ceremony of the anointing of the sick for that afternoon, and although we had received several calls earlier in the day asking us to postpone since people would not be able to travel, it was too late to do so as I knew many would already be on their way.

As it turned out, over a hundred people came. I have carried out many such ceremonies, but this was the first time I told those who attended that I too was there as one of the sick.

It was very emotional to be anointed for the first time, alongside so many people carrying all kinds of illnesses. It was almost like it was meant to happen that the ceremony should fall at the end of this particular week.

We read a piece about Jesus healing. I have often wondered about the mystery of healing, and I wondered again that day. Would it happen to me? Would I be healed? Or would healing happen in another, more unexpected, way?

It was to be a busy day. Later that evening I met up with three priest friends, Charlie, Declan and John, whom I had met in the seminary. We have met up, the three of us, almost every Sunday night for the last twenty-seven years. We have moved from pub to hotel to pub trying to find a place to talk and especially to listen to one another. These meetings have sustained us over the years, through all the ups and downs we have experienced in the priesthood and in our own lives. They are very faithful friends and we have often had wonderful holidays together.

Over the years, we've gone from having a couple of

beers on these Sunday nights, to now drinking tea and talking about what colour tablets we are taking. How times have changed! However, these are moments where we can just be ourselves and can speak openly to one another.

This particular Sunday night they were shocked to hear my news, but gave me the time to talk about everything that had happened over the last few days. It was great to see them and feel the full weight of a support that has been there for such a long time.

In those first few days I tried so hard to be strong and positive – for my own sake, but also for those around me.

And as parishioners, friends and family rallied around, I felt Jesus powerfully. Surely to love and be loved is the greatest longing within the human spirit and soul. I reminded myself, as I stood looking out at the white world over those devastating days, that I am deeply loved, and that I, in turn, have always tried to love. And that I have made every effort to overcome the greatest hurdle of all – which is to be able to say that I have loved myself, in all the shades of light and darkness.

Sermon – Easter Vigil 2011

In the gospel the women arrive at the tomb, confused and sad. They had seen Jesus crucified and the other disciples running away afraid. However, they come to anoint the body of Jesus and instead discover that he has risen from the dead. Perhaps as they were leaving they remembered that Jesus had promised that he would rise from the dead after three days. They might also have been thinking that the others would never believe them. But here he is, Jesus, in front of them urging them to have no fear. What a change has happened between their arriving at the tomb and leaving it.

The same Jesus is with us in all times of trouble and doubt. He says these words to us too: 'Do not be afraid.' It is sometimes difficult to believe this and I'm sure some of the disciples would not have believed it until they saw Jesus for themselves. Many times we feel our prayers are not even heard, never mind answered. And yet we find a way to keep going and I suggest sometimes that when we look back we will see that our prayers have been answered, just not in the way we expected. The disciples never expected to see Jesus on the beach eating fish with them in a later appearance.

What is certain is that the promise made by Jesus was kept. He did rise from the dead. Because of this, death is defeated, meaning that the end of our life will not be that. We shall live because Jesus lives.

We then can be a people who hope against hope and we need to encourage each other to have that hope even in the darkest days. If we who believe do not show this hope in our lives, how can we expect others to believe it is possible?

Early Faith

When I was a child, my parents used to say the rosary with us, as a family. As children do, we would often mess and giggle, until we got a stern look. Despite the messing, I believe those hours spent praying together are what formed the basis of my own spiritual life, and I know that all my faith is predicated on what Jesus says and does.

While I always felt Jesus' presence as a very real part of my life, the decision to begin training for the priesthood wasn't an easy one. I was used to the working world, taking on jobs in order to contribute to our household and to help my mother. My first summer job, when I was fifteen, was in a pub in Christchurch, Dublin, bringing drinks to customers' tables and clearing up when they left. I enjoyed the work but remember a specific incident when a new manager told me at the end of a night that my till was short twenty pounds and that there'd be trouble if I didn't make up the balance. I was only making forty pounds a week, but I asked my mother for a loan and I gave the manager the twenty. A few weeks later the owner called me into her office and asked if I had ever given the manager any money. I told her my story. It turned out that the manager had been stealing from the pub and covering it up by getting money from the junior members of staff. He was duly sacked.

The following summer I worked as a porter at the Crofton Airport Hotel on the Swords Road. At that stage it was owned by the Reagan family. Every evening, old Mr Reagan would go to his own apartment within the hotel, and as he went he turned off all the lights. The hotel had more than a whiff of Fawlty Towers about it.

I remember one time I brought up breakfast for the

singer Hazel O'Connor. I knocked on the door and she asked me to come in. I placed the breakfast tray on a counter opposite the bed, but as I headed to the door I heard an almighty crash. The breakfast had fallen onto the floor. I went back to pick it up but Hazel was already doing it and said, 'Don't worry about it.' So, instead, I asked her for an autograph and went down to the kitchen to get her a new pot of tea.

I enjoyed working there more than in the pub, as I met such a range of characters from all over the world. The only disadvantage was carrying their cases on a day when the lifts didn't work, and there was rarely a day when the lifts were fully operational. But there were advantages too – if I was in a room and a customer asked me a question I didn't know the answer to, I would tell them to phone reception, knowing full well that the phones were often out of order.

After completing my Leaving Certificate in 1982, I did a business administration course and as part of my placement I worked in the credit control department of the *Irish Independent*. The 'Indo' was full of wise-cracking characters who on the surface appeared grumpy but who were actually genuinely lovely and helpful people. I can't remember what exactly I did there, but I certainly learned nothing about credit control.

On completing the course I was called for interview for the position of property title researcher in a solicitor's office, with the promise that I would quickly progress to a more permanent role in law. Instead, however, I took a job in the public service at the General Medical Services Payments Board which was based in Finglas. We needed money at home and I convinced myself that the permanence of the medical board job would be the better option.

While all this was going on, a local priest in our parish in Iona Road in Glasnevin, Father Des Forristal, told my mother about a young adult group he was forming in the parish and asked if I'd be interested in joining. My mother told him that I would. Throughout my childhood, we often had priests or nuns staying at our house, sleeping on the couch or on the floor. One of the more colourful and larger-than-life characters was Sister Evangelist, who wore a long veil and a habit with a large set of rosary beads hanging from a belt. She had been on the missions in Africa for many years and was an enthusiastic and formidable character.

Then there was my father's brother, Anthony, who was ordained as a Divine Word Missionary priest in 1972. He was initially appointed to Argentina during the years of the military dictatorship. He used to write me letters on thin blue airmail paper that he would seal around the edges. He wrote on every available inch of the paper in tiny writing. In these letters, he told me about his work in Argentina, his mission among the poor and the threats made to priests and the religious orders from the government. Every couple of years he came back to Ireland and stayed with us. He was a big influence on me in many ways.

One of the heroes to our family when my father left was a priest from our local parish who regularly brought us food hampers. He drank a lot and often looked very pale, but he had a kind and compassionate heart. On the day of the delivery he would have a cup of tea with my mother and smoke a cigarette. I often feel that these chats with my mother dispelled for a short time the loneliness he felt. I think of him often and of the example he set for me that I've often emulated during my own ministry as a priest.

I used to see Father Forristal going around on his bicycle visiting parishioners. I admired his effort to be with the people, and the gentleness he showed to all those with problems.

I could see the effect these people had on the community and how they treated everyone they met with compassion and kindness. So while initially I wasn't happy with my mother's suggestion that I join Father

Forristal and the youth group, I was aware of the good that a priest can do in a community and I also wanted to keep the peace at home. So I agreed to go along and check it out.

That was a lucky move because I met a really lovely group of people around my own age and also a little older. These were the first friends I had made in several years. As a family we were still struggling after my father left and I keenly felt the responsibility of being the eldest boy – in terms of trying to earn money but also being there for my mother and my brothers. In a way, I had become quite isolated. I had grown up long before my time but the young adult group with Father Forristal allowed me space and an opportunity to loosen up and enjoy life a bit more.

Father Forristal organised meetings in his house where we discussed different aspects of faith. We also had weekend trips away to Glendalough and other parts of the country and learned to party together. That group, built on a common ground of faith and prayer, was a great mixture of reflection, friendship and social interaction. I was grateful that he had brought us all together.

I had always been driven by two things – wanting to do good for others, and wanting, like everyone, to be happy in life. Watching Father Forristal, I began to think, *I'd love to be like him; he's an amazing man.* I know people who became teachers because of the influence of a particular teacher of their own – it was a bit like that.

But it wasn't all straightforward. I wanted to work to earn money for the family and I was also troubled by the sacrifices of a priest's life. I wrestled with the decision again and again in my head, often pushing it away and not wanting to deal with it because, along with seeing the value of a priest's life, I was also developing a strong connection with one member of the young adult group – a girl I became very close to. She was a beautiful singer and harpist, and I suppose we just clicked from the outset.

This began a period of great turmoil as I tried to figure out what I should do. One day I went to see Father Forristal to ask his advice. He told me that if I was meant to be a priest, God would keep after me until I said yes. There was no pressure from Father Forristal at all.

The call to religious life was persistent, and no matter what I did, I couldn't get it out of my head. But at the same time the group kept on meeting, and I fell more and more in love with the girl.

In the end, I made the decision in a way that was unusual, but at the same time very ordinary.

At evening mass one day in Iona Road Church, in front

of me was an elderly man, neatly dressed in a suit, shirt and tie, though the shirt was quite dirty and rumpled, so I got the impression he might be struggling financially. At the end of the mass a hymn was sung, and the man joined in at the top of his voice, even though he hadn't a note in his head.

I observed his effort, and I took it as a sign: if that man could put so much into demonstrating his love and commitment to God, then I would give the priesthood a try.

By then, the idea had begun to overwhelm me. I still had strong feelings for the girl in our group but the call to religious life in the service of God and others gripped me – as a way of life more than a job. I felt compelled to explore it, so I said to myself, 'Okay, I'll give it a try.'

In a way, this was an answer to my prayers, but I had yet to tell the girl. When I did, she was annoyed and very upset, but I must say she eventually found love with a wonderful husband and great children. I was at her wedding, and she and her husband were at my ordination. I never intended to hurt her. The whole idea of priesthood overwhelmed me, and from then on I was determined to give it a go.

And so, on 14 September 1985, aged twenty-one, together with thirteen other men, I entered Holy Cross

College in Clonliffe, Dublin to begin training for the priesthood. We were all asked to be there at a particular time and so it resembled the first day of term at a boarding school when all the children arrive at once, with parents and family. I was accompanied by my mother and Kieran and Pat. When I told Mam of my decision, she was delighted. 'If it doesn't work out,' she said, 'don't worry.' But she was very happy, very supportive. Even still, I was full of nerves and it felt strange, moving from home to this place. There were a couple of speeches and then we were shown to our rooms where we had a bed, a desk, a chair and a sink.

When the families began to leave, my mother and I couldn't find Pat or Kieran. Students from other years began to search the building and eventually found them in the basement. Kieran was playing on the snooker table and Pat was sitting on a big chair in which Pope John Paul II had sat during mass in the Phoenix Park in 1979. To them, this was an adventure but at the time I must admit I wanted to kill them both. Now we were known as the family with the two boys who went missing. My family were the last to leave that day.

In all, I spent six years training for the priesthood – studying theology and philosophy and doing pastoral work in Saint Michael's House, the school for the deaf in

Cabra, and Saint Patrick's Institute for young offenders. In the summer of 1989 I spent three months in the Mater Hospital doing a CPE (clinical pastoral education). I did it with a fellow student from my seminary, and about seven other religious from all over Ireland. Our group was led by Sister Louisa Richie, Medical Missionaries of Mary (MMM), a kind and very astute facilitator.

The object of the training was to learn skills that would enable us to reach out pastorally to patients in the hospital. We had duty time where we visited the wards and talked to patients. I loved the evenings, when all the visitors were gone home. In the old Mater Hospital, patients would sit out on the corridor or on the wide windowsills, and I still remember a fireman called Tony who was living with cancer. His prognosis was not good, and I recall listening to him talking about the love he had for his wife and children and his readiness to die. He had piercing eyes that lent conviction to what he said. I learned from him that this pastoral outreach was about listening a lot and talking very little. He never asked me for answers, and anyway I wouldn't have had any to give him. He enriched my time in the hospital, as did a young boy called Thomas who spent long periods there. He always called out to me when he saw me and I had many good chats with him and his parents. They were all at my ordination in 1991, at which stage Thomas was better and no longer in hospital.

From 1990 to 1991 I spent time in Donaghmede parish. The new parish priest, Jim Moriarty, was my contact. Every Tuesday I had tea with him, prepared by his housekeeper Mary. I got involved with local schools, and one day Father Moriarty said, 'There's a women's group who meet regularly, they want to know will you join them?' So I did, and together we discussed many issues in our lives. These women talked about everything, including their husbands and their families, and I often felt like a little boy in this group – they had so many life experiences, and between them about twenty children. I learned so much about family life from them.

One evening, one of the women said that the thing that kept her awake at night was that she'd had a stillborn baby, and the child was in limbo. I asked her what she meant. I had never heard of limbo. Now I know that it originated from a debate between Saint Augustine and Pelagius about original sin: are babies born with original sin? Where do they go if they are unbaptised? But at the time I knew nothing about it so I asked what she meant.

She said, 'My child is not in heaven yet.'

'I don't believe that,' I replied. 'I think your child is an angel.'

Anyone who believes in the God of love knows that those children go to heaven and they are angels, but some ignorant priest had told this woman her child would be forever in limbo; neither here, nor there. Horrible things were said to people in those days.

Happily, she believed me. She burst out crying and we couldn't say another word for the rest of us were all crying as well.

Also in the parish I began to preach every Sunday. My homilies were always short, mainly because I could see the effort parents had made to bring their children to mass and I knew even then that long sermons bore everyone, particularly children!

The parish priest was also keen that we would go out and visit families in their homes, and so together with the other priests we did this regularly. One night I knocked on a door wearing my clerical collar. The young man who opened was wearing only a towel and had money in his hand. The woman on the stairs behind him called out, 'Is that it?' They were waiting for a pizza! Naturally enough I didn't stick around.

And I was never really one for the clerical collar. I remember soon after my ordination – I was only ordained a few days – a friend of mine called for me and I came downstairs in jeans and a t-shirt. My mother said, 'Are you going out dressed like that?'

'Mam, I am,' I replied. 'Get used to it.'

And she did. She would often say to me, 'Are you not wearing your collar today?'

I'd say no, and that was the end of it. I know there are people who wear the suit and the collar – and I think they look like goons! In the modern world no one wears a badge to say what they are, so why should we? My mother soon accepted that I wasn't going to be quite the type of priest she had expected.

I realised during my training that my calling – and where I was happiest – was out in the community helping people and living the word of love and the gospels. And happily, after I was ordained a priest by Bishop Kavanagh on 7 June 1991 in Iona Road Church, I was sent to Ballymun, which was one of the strongest communities I could have been placed in, as chaplain in the Comprehensive secondary school in Ballymun and as chaplain to the Sisters of Charity in Drumcondra.

Ballymun Years

In the early 1990s, Ballymun was an area of high unemployment and afflicted by a chronic drug problem. The school, a secondary school for boys and girls, known locally as 'The Comp', was situated before the large roundabout in Ballymun and I arrived there as chaplain on the first day of term in late August 1991. Mr Marren, the principal, introduced me to the staff. My heart was thumping. I didn't know what to say or do but within minutes people were shaking my hand and welcoming me and saying they hoped I would be happy there.

Many of the staff had been in the school since they graduated from college and most of them were in their late thirties and early forties. It was the beginning of what was to be a wonderful nine years in Ballymun.

Later on that first day, Mr Marren told me that the father of one of the teachers had died and he asked me if I would like to go with him to Donegal the next day for the funeral. I said I would. I hadn't even met that particular teacher yet. Mr Marren's car was immaculate, in contrast to my own. It turned out that he knew my parents from many years ago when he was working in the VEC (Vocational Education Committee) where my father also worked. He said he remembered them from dinner dances.

At the funeral, it suddenly dawned on me that another of the deceased man's sons had been my science teacher in secondary school. They say Ireland is a small place and if proof were needed, on this journey I made two connections from the past. Mr Marren was a kind man, an old-style school principal. He was respectful and interested and always asked me if I was okay.

Barely a year later, on 1 April 1992, Mr Marren came into my office to make sure the room was warm enough.

I told him it was fine. 'I don't know,' he said, 'I feel a bit chilly.' That day he was due to attend a principals and vice principals conference, but just a few minutes later another teacher, Gerry Hoey, ran in and said, 'Something's up with Mr Marren!' We ran down to his office and saw him slumped at his desk, but there was no response when we called to him. Myself and Aidan, a teacher at the school, and as it happens a former priest, placed him lying on the floor and Aidan tried to give him mouth-to-mouth resuscitation.

The ambulance came quickly, and as they took Mr Marren away I heard one of the paramedics say, 'He's dead.' I followed the ambulance to the Mater Hospital's emergency department and when I got there a nurse told me Mr Marren had died. I was in shock. I saw that his wife and daughter were outside and so I had to rally myself, for their sake. There is no perfect way to tell someone such news so I said simply, 'Mrs Marren, I'm very sorry but Mr Marren died a few minutes ago.' She literally slumped to the floor as her daughter tried to hold her up.

I have always found that being a priest allows you to enter the sacred space of others. As well as being a privilege, this can also be difficult, as words are often insufficient in the midst of life's important moments. But I have found that gesture and touch can take the place of words, and can bring some warmth even in the coldest situations.

My routine in those days was that I said 7.30 a.m. mass every Monday to Friday in the Sisters of Charity convent in Drumcondra, and at 10 a.m. on a Sunday. Most of the sisters had retired by then. Every morning after mass we would have boiled eggs and toast, and tea or coffee, with mine served to me on my own in a small parlour. Eventually I requested that I have breakfast with the nuns.

After mass on weekdays, I went to the Comp. I had an office in the school and a few teaching hours of religion. The young boys and girls used to tell me, 'Father Tony, you are a sound man!' This was a great compliment and you would have to do something very serious to mess up that affection. Generally, these young people were honest and forthright. One year, a uniform was introduced for the first time. This was mainly driven by a sense of fairness and equality: some children could afford better clothes than others, so those who couldn't afford good clothes were often laughed at. The staff agreed that the pupils must wear the full uniform and each teacher should enforce this in their own classroom. One day I was calling the roll in my class. One of the boys was not wearing his tie so as I continued calling the roll, I said, 'Stephen, please put on your tie.'

He answered sharply, 'I will in a minute.'

I said, 'Do it now!' and when I asked him again he told me to 'F**k off'. I said to him, 'Stephen, go down to the principal's office and tell him I want to see your father.' So often, it was the mothers who came down to the school, called out for every disciplinary problem, and I didn't think it was fair that they had to bear all the responsibility for their children, which was why I asked for Stephen's father.

The next day, Stephen duly arrived with his father, who said, 'Father Tony, I'm really sorry. That language was inexcusable.' Then he turned to his son. 'Tell Father Tony you're f**kin' sorry!'

I burst out laughing and told Stephen to go back into the classroom. I realised early on that what was called 'bad language' was in common usage, and Stephen's father honestly didn't know what I found so funny. In fairness to Stephen, he was always a good student and I got on with him very well after that.

I soon realised that I could do nothing to convince young people to stay away from drugs. Their peers were much more powerful. There were deaths from drugs during my years in Ballymun, and other fallout too. One day the sister of one of our first-year students died by suicide, after jumping from one of the flats. We brought this boy's whole class to her funeral. When we were leaving, some of the children were crying. One of the boys reached out and took my hand. I was aware that people on a bus stopped opposite the church saw me, a priest, holding a child's hand. I saw them staring, but I resolved not to let go because that child was reaching out for care in a moment of distress. He held tightly as we walked back to school.

Truancy was a big problem, and many times both myself and the home–school liaison teacher were called on to intervene. Sometimes this went well, often not. One boy we persuaded to come back is now a professor at NUI Galway. He came from a home where the family had very, very little – I went to call at Christmas one year, and there was nothing in that house. No decorations, no presents, no food. His sister became a drug addict, his brother dropped out of school, but that boy, had something inside him. He was a real star.

When it came time for him to go to third-level, I suggested Galway rather than UCD –there was a stigma attached to Ballymun, and he would have stuck out like a sore thumb in UCD, but I knew he wouldn't even be noticed in Galway.

We called to see another boy who had been doing very well in school but had stopped going. Now, the central heating in the flats was centrally controlled. It was either on or off, but you couldn't individually regulate it. So I went into this flat and it was roasting and everyone was in their underwear, even the parents. The dad said, 'Father, do you want to take something off?' That was a funny moment, but sadly the boy never came back to school. I suppose maybe his parents didn't value it.

In the Comp, there were many challenges for the very committed staff but there were also opportunities. There had been no school outing abroad for many years so myself and five other teachers decided to advertise a trip to Paris. Luckily, Mary, the French teacher, was willing to come. Sixty young people aged between twelve and fifteen signed up for the trip. To make things more manageable, we divided them into groups of ten so that wherever we were, each of the teachers had their own small(ish) group. On the first day we brought them to the Louvre. Not long after our arrival an alarm went off and I thought to myself, 'Please God, no!', but sure enough, when I looked around, a lady who worked there was shouting something in French to three of our charges. Also, in the middle of the melee was Mary, trying to placate the museum worker.

It turned out that the boys had put their arms around a bust on a plinth in order to take a photograph. As soon as they touched it, the alarm went off. Anyway, we escaped with just a warning.

We toured the palace of Versailles in about twenty minutes. The children ran from one end to another. We tried to point out some of the beauty of the building, but we were talking to ourselves. So we cut our losses and got out of there.

We had also booked a trip to a fantastic water park outside Paris and when our time was up there, no one wanted to leave. Most of them had never been on a plane before or had never travelled abroad. For most, too, this was the first time on holidays without their parents.

We teachers used to flop into chairs in the foyer each night and have a glass of wine and a great chat while reminiscing on the day's events. The trip proved a huge success, and we were very glad we'd taken it on. More importantly, we returned with sixty students!

Also at the school we set up the Rainbows Programme, for children whose parents had separated or if one or both had died. Ann, the home–school liaison teacher, and I each facilitated a group. For most of the children, this was the first time they talked about how they felt in relation to events in their family life. What was very touching was the way they listened to and supported each other in those little groups. Children are often the forgotten mourners at funerals or indeed during and after their parents' separation. I could relate to these children at a personal level and, in a way, I would love to have had the opportunity when I was that age to be in a group like this. That was what made me so passionate about introducing Rainbows into the school.

One very rewarding moment was when we invited the parents to come to a certificate presentation when the children had completed the programme. Some of the students got up and talked about the experience of being in the group. There were tears, but much laughter too as these parents saw a light return to their children which had been missing for some time.

I found myself directing school musicals such as *The King and I*, *Fiddler on the Roof* and *Grease*. I had no experience of this but some of the children had been in musicals before and so I took their advice on how to be the director.

We had boys and girls from the age of twelve to eighteen singing and acting on the school stage to a sell-out crowd every night, something they would never had dreamed of. The teachers got involved in building the sets, designing costumes and doing make-up. More students from the school took part in stage production, selling programmes and, of course, raffle tickets. These were marvellous times of creativity, fun, and the realisation of wonderful talent in our students.

On the last night of each show, I held a party in my house for the teachers and the main leads, who were all sixth-year students. We sang the songs from the show, following which Leo, the local postman, became our DJ!

My main inspiration in all this was the incredible potential of young people. It's something that has never left me, and I always cherished the opportunity to speak to these young people before they went out into the world.

I could relate numerous other stories from my days in Ballymun, but I think it is enough to say that I learned so much there. Despite the very obvious hardship, I will never forget the strength of the community – and it's this sense of community which has become so important to me now in my illness. People always rallied around at times of loss or hardship, and were also there during moments of joy and celebration. The mothers worked very hard – you would see them being picked up in vans at the roundabout and taken to cleaning jobs all over Dublin – while many of the fathers were unemployed. Those women were amazing – they had really tough lives, but they managed. And they were very supportive of the school.

Despite the reputation Ballymun had then, I was never afraid. I felt I could go anywhere. I also found that

I could achieve far more as a priest in that area than, for example, a social worker could. I remember a woman whose husband beat her and threw her out of the house. The guards were called, and so was I, and the guards wanted her to press charges but she said to me, 'I can't, Father. I love him.'

'I don't believe in that kind of love,' I replied. And I didn't. I don't believe in love that gives you a punch. But I do believe in telling the truth.

She did finally press charges. It took several weeks and another bad beating, but she did it.

After six years in Ballymun, the bishop suggested a move, but I asked for two more years and he agreed. After all, as the gospel says, 'Ask and you shall receive.'

In fact, I stayed for another three years. Then one evening I received a call asking me to become a chaplain at UCD. Initially I was reluctant, but my good friends said it would really suit me and I should give it a go. So with a heavy heart I left Ballymun.

As a priest, you know you have limited time in any one place. From the outside, this might seem cruel – especially when you are very happy and settled. But it is the life I chose, and so in the summer of 2000 I left Ballymun to take up my new position as one of the chaplains at University College Dublin.

The Beginning of an Idea

Shortly after my first diagnosis, I was given an appointment to meet Professor Orla Hardiman, a consultant neurologist, at Beaumont hospital in March 2018. By that time, my left leg was less mobile and I dragged it a bit, and my left hand was closing so that I had not much mobility in my fingers. But I was still able to drive and walk around unaided. My cousin John drove me to the appointment, however, and on arrival I was registered as a patient. This was a very strange feeling because I had never been in hospital as a patient, only to visit the sick. I was very nervous that day.

We walked down a corridor so crowded that it reminded me of a railway platform when passengers disembark from a train. Our clinic was the last on the corridor. Once there, we sat on the hard wooden seats, many without armrests, that are provided for patients. It struck me that there wasn't even a table, so anything we had in our hands, we had to put on the floor. Not for the first time, I thought about how little care and dignity is sometimes afforded to patients.

Eventually, Orla Hardiman was free and we went in to meet her, along with the MND nurse, Bernie, and another nurse, Katie.

Orla instantly began chatting about her love of Saint Augustine and, as we have done many times since, we sparred briefly over theological matters. The following November we were to appear on *The Late Late Show* together to raise awareness about MND, during which she said of our first meeting, 'We had a great conversation that day. I kind of like church history and have an interest in history, so I was testing out his history of theology but he won.'

Orla examined me briefly and confirmed that it was motor neurone disease, which at that stage we hoped might be mild.

There was great warmth in the room that day, much laughter and honesty. I felt I was being listened to and I also felt more positive about my diagnosis. I had thought myself that my MND might be mild, and now I had the care of someone I felt I could trust. The meeting reaffirmed my inner resolve not to be defeated.

Already an idea was forming in my mind – something that would give me focus. It involved doing a fundraising walk. The Chaplaincy team in UCD, which I joined in 2000, led many initiatives within the university, including the UCD Choral Scholars, an annual fashion show for charity, and the Student Hardship Fund. On arrival I decided to help out with as many charities as I could. I mentioned my idea that day to Orla and the team, and someone – I can't remember who exactly – said to me that what I needed to do was take my time and rest. I thought to myself, 'You don't know me.'

Before we left, I met a physiotherapist and an occupational therapist. And that was the end of day one as a registered patient. It had been a very long day: we had arrived at 10.30 a.m. and didn't leave until 3.45 p.m.

At that point, I started thinking that if the illness was mild, maybe it would progress slowly and I would have many years in which I could function without much difficulty. I remember feeling upbeat following that meeting and especially about the idea of the walk, which I felt would allow me to do something positive, and would give me a focus. I decided it was time to be more open about what was happening, so I wrote a piece in the newsletters of Mount Merrion and Kilmacud, the two parishes that I administer, telling people about my diagnosis.

25th March 2018

Firstly, I would like to thank everyone for your care and concern as I have been 'hobbling' around for some time! I have been very moved by the cards, prayers and the many candles that have been lit as some of the expressions of that care. Two weeks ago I was diagnosed with motor neurone disease. It was an awful shock that terrified me. And as some of that shock continues to reside in my body it is accompanied by a desire to live, to face life looking forward, in the knowledge that this is a new turn on the road of my personal journey but one I do not travel alone. The love of my family, friends and parishioners will be the fuel of my daily living. I intend to continue ministering in the parishes as best I can for as long as I can. As you will understand I won't have daily reports as to how I am getting on! I want to live as normally as possible. Please do say a few prayers for me as it is ultimately into the hands of a compassionate and merciful God, whom I love, that I place myself.

Fr Tony

Despite my positivity, however, I could see how the illness, even if mild and progressing slowly, would affect my life, and that was going to be one of the hardest things to cope with.

My Time at UCD

I have never been someone who just gives out about something without trying to make it better. In the charities I was involved with in UCD, I saw at first hand the effect that being active in ministry could have. My first real experience of this was in 2002, two years after I arrived at the university.

That year, two students came to my office asking if

I knew any overseas charity that would allow them and their peers to volunteer abroad during the summer. At that stage I was also chaplain to a convent in Goatstown, the Sisters of Jesus and Mary. One of the sisters there, Marie, told me that they had contacts in India and Haiti. I emailed both contacts and Haiti responded first, and eventually India.

There was a civil war raging in Haiti at the time, so I thought it might not be the best place for the students. Instead, driven by their enthusiasm, I decided to advertise a volunteer trip to Delhi for July 2003. I outlined my idea to the student advisor, Aoife Fitzgerald, whose office was beside mine in the science building. She was very supportive, and that July Aoife and I led a group of twenty-two students from a range of faculties across the university, to India. As soon as we left the airport building in Delhi, we hit a wall of heat, even though it was only early morning. I'd never experienced anything like it. Within a short time our clothes were wet and sweat was running down our backs. The heat was so intense, you could smell it.

It was still early in the morning when we arrived at a hostel and I happily climbed into bed. After what seemed like only a couple of hours there was a knock on the door to tell me I was wanted downstairs. I went down with Aoife to meet our contact, Sunita, who explained that the students would work on a range of projects, including an orphanage run by the Missionaries of Charity, which was founded by Mother Teresa. They would help to build a sports ground in a slum area and work in another orphanage called Salaam Baalak. I was amazed how quickly our students got stuck in to their various projects. I was also amazed at their confidence. I was comparing myself to them at their age and thinking I was never so confident. The following year I brought another group to Delhi, this time over thirty students.

Then in December of the same year I went to Haiti for the first time, alone, to assess it as a possible destination for our overseas volunteers. It proved to be an eventful trip. At Dublin airport my flight to New York was delayed because of damage to the plane, so after a night in a hotel I got going the next day, first to New York and from there to Port-au-Prince in Haiti. Because of the delay, the people who had come to meet me had long gone. My mobile phone didn't work there so I couldn't ring anyone. Crowds of people were standing around shouting 'taxi' and others were trying to grab my bag.

Eventually a taxi driver with very good English approached me. I asked him if he could get me to a hotel with email. We arrived at a small hotel where I could check my email for one dollar. I found the telephone number I needed on my email and phoned it from the hotel phone. Sister Jackie answered and gave directions to the taxi man.

When we pulled up at our destination, a convent in Port-au-Prince, the driver locked all the doors and asked me for fifty dollars. At that stage, I was so weary I just gave him the money.

That was my first meeting with Sister Jackie, a Sister of Jesus and Mary, who had been working in Gros Morne for nearly twenty years. We headed straight to Gros Morne on what was to be a five-hour car journey over dreadful roads. Driving the car was Tiden, who had worked with the sisters for many years. He seemed to know everyone along the road and drove while drinking a bottle of Prestige, the local beer.

I met Sister Pat and some other American volunteers who were there for a year. The sisters said they were willing to take a group the following July, and showed me work that could be done in the nearby mountains to prevent flooding, the hospital where medical students could work, and a home for elderly people that needed renovation. The sisters would also provide suitable accommodation for the volunteer group. I fell in love with Haiti that day. The people were warm and friendly, but the searing poverty was evident everywhere and I knew there would be plenty of work for our student volunteers.

In 2006 I travelled to Nicaragua to look at another potential project. One of our previous volunteers in Haiti had an aunt who knew a Nicaraguan doctor in Ireland. This doctor in turn knew Doctor Margarita Gurdián, who at the time was Minister for Health in Nicaragua, and he told me there were projects in Nicaragua that she could help me identify.

So I flew to Managua and was met by Doctor Gurdián and two of her staff. Each day, two doctors brought me to different villages to see the work they were doing, but I became increasingly embarrassed as I knew we could not help with these particular projects, because they required skills and expertise our volunteers didn't have, and I had very little Spanish with which to explain what it was we could do.

On the last day of my trip, we drove to a town called Somoto in northern Nicaragua, on the border with Honduras. There we met an American volunteer, Alison, who was fluent in Spanish. At last, I had someone who would translate for me.

I met with the village council, made up of men and women of all ages, and asked them what they needed. They said a health centre, water for the village and, possibly because I was a priest, painting the church. That day, I made a promise that we would help.

In 2007, when we returned, our group of student volunteers built a wonderful health centre; one of my proudest days was when we hired a drill to look for water. Nearly the entire village was out on the road, digging trenches for the pipes that would bring the water to where it was needed. That was the beginning of several years' involvement in that area, during which time we worked with the villagers to improve living conditions and healthcare.

I could see at first hand what positive action can achieve for people. The real answer to poverty and distress is a question, 'What am I doing to alleviate it in the world?' Pope Francis insinuated that it's not good enough to go to mass on Sunday and on the way home pass by a homeless person. Since I was ordained, I have tried to listen to the words of Isaiah, read by Jesus: 'The Spirit of the Lord is on me, because he has anointed me to proclaim good news to the poor. He has sent me to proclaim freedom for the prisoners and recovery of sight for the blind, to set the oppressed free' (Luke 4:18). Too many people complain about the world and do nothing to make a difference. Christians who truly live their faith are never bystanders; rather, they are the ones who seek to respond to the needs of the poor and the oppressed.

Faith is not just about attending mass. Many of the young people who do are also involved in voluntary work at home and abroad. Others who may have given up attending mass do many good deeds for their neighbours and friends, so I believe that when we talk about the 'practice' of faith, we need to broaden how we view that, and see it through a far wider lens than simply attendance at Sunday mass.

Around the time of my first meeting with Professor Hardiman, I heard a radio interview with Doddie Weir, who used to play rugby for Scotland. He too lives with MND, and he said that the drug administered to those with the illness is called Rilutek, and that this has been the case for twenty-four years – there have been little new research findings or treatments in that time. I knew too that there were only three dedicated MND nurses working in Ireland, with almost four hundred sufferers, and that these nurses were paid by voluntary contributions or church gate collections.

And so it was that I began to think about a fundraising walk, something that would raise awareness about MND and raise funds for research and care for those affected.

Walk Preparation and a New Set of Wheels

As the idea for the walk took shape, and driven by the gradual, but noticeable, progression of my illness, I met two of my former UCD colleagues with whom I had stayed in touch – even though I had left UCD ten years before – guidance counsellors Aoife and Joe, and told them of my plans. They were very enthusiastic from the start and said they would love to be involved and would do whatever was needed to make it a success. I wasn't surprised, as both are great at getting things done.

I next contacted a teacher in one of our parish schools, Naoise Maguire. He said he would love to be part of the walk and I asked him to plan the route on Google Maps. He said he wasn't sure how to do this and I said to him, 'I know, but you'll figure it out.'

I contacted Johnny Blackmore, whom I had known as a student in UCD. He is a whizz with design and formatting of material online. I asked him if he would design a website, and even though he said he'd never done it before, he uttered the eternal words 'Leave it with me.'

Leslie Buckley provided staff from his Haiti-based NGO Haven, who gave us advice on logistics and the organisation of such a big event. All this was the beginning of the adventure that would become Walk While You Can (the name came from Leanne, one of my fellow-students when I was later training to be a psychotherapist, and we all felt it was perfect: invitational rather than judgmental). As I write, the project has so far raised nearly €700,000 for MND research and care.

I knew we would need publicity to get this venture off the ground, so I contacted Roger Childs in RTÉ. Roger is editor of religious programmes and some years previously had filmed the Saint Thérèse Christmas Day Family Mass. I asked him if he had any contacts with *The Ryan Tubridy Show*, because I often listen to it in the morning. I always find Ryan to be patient with his guests and he gives them plenty of time to say what they're saying. I felt then that if I was given time on the show, I would have the opportunity to talk about the walk and why we were doing it.

Roger said he'd do his best, and after a few days I received a call from Susan, a researcher with the show. After a long conversation, she told me she would get back to me with a possible date, and I subsequently heard that I'd be on the show on Thursday, 19 April. On that day, Susan met me at the door of the radio centre in RTÉ and took me upstairs to a waiting area. I remember it being a beautiful balmy day, and I was delighted to be given water, coffee and a nice pastry.

Once I was brought in to meet Ryan, he gave me a very warm handshake and told me to remember that this was just a chat and that I was to relax. His advice turned out to be excellent, and I completely forgot that there was a microphone on the table. I spoke about issues relating to my illness, my early family life and the walk, and there was an overwhelming response to my interview.

I was totally humbled and thrilled with the goodwill

and messages of support from so many people. What was even more exciting was that, three days after being on the show, we had already raised €35,000!

But as plans for the walk got underway with much enthusiasm, my condition began to decline. Initially I used a walking stick to help my balance. I thought this might feel a bit weird at my age, fifty-three, but I found the stick helped me, and that was all that mattered. I was also still driving at this stage, and when saying mass in Mount Merrion and Kilmacud I received great help from the sacristans at both churches, Michael and Kevin, who helped me in and out of the car. It took me so long to walk from one side of the sanctuary to the other that I could feel the congregation holding their collective breath, and letting it go in relief once I sat down without falling!

Around this time, at one of my regular appointments, Professor Hardiman said she couldn't believe I was still walking – and that I shouldn't be, that it wasn't safe.

I began to realise that such was the weakness by then, particularly in my left leg, I would need a wheelchair for some of the time. I happened to mention this to a young parishioner as we chatted one day, and within hours she phoned me to say that her parents would like to buy me a wheelchair. The one I had in mind was available on

Amazon. It was relatively light, could be folded in half to go in the boot of a car, and, most importantly, it was electronic, which meant that I, with the help of a small joystick, could drive it myself. This was very important to me in an effort to maintain my independence.

The diocese agreed to renovate my home, meaning that my garage and utility room would now become my bedroom and wet room, giving me total access to the downstairs. In addition, my brother Pat and his wife Michelle – I married them, which was a great thrill – said I would be welcome to stay in their home in Ballinteer, and so their spare room downstairs, which normally housed a computer and my nephew Oscar's piano, became my bedroom for the next six weeks. My eldest nephew Rían donated (or was made to donate!) his bed and moved in with his brother. I had a great time there; it was a very easy-going household. I remember with happiness World Cup soccer matches in the afternoon with my youngest nephew, seven-year-old Mikey. Before each game he would tell me who the best players were on each team and what he felt the score would be. He and I had the simple happiness of being together, doing something we both enjoyed.

At that stage I was able to shower and dress myself, except for putting on my socks and shoes. But one night I had a very bad fall on the way to the bathroom. I literally fell face down, but I fell on my walking stick, landing on my ribs. There was only Micky in the house at the time and he was in bed asleep. I had to wait for my brother and sister-in-law to come back. They tried to get me up, but couldn't. Michelle went to a house a few doors down and asked for help. Someone had the brainwave of putting a sheet under me and lifting it and me together into the wheelchair.

My ribs were very painful, so my brother brought me to the Swiftcare clinic in Balally. When the nurse saw my hand I explained I had motor neurone disease. 'That is absolutely shit,' she said, 'to have this fall on top of that awful illness.' I loved her directness.

A doctor came in then and spent a good while examining my arm, even though I kept telling her that it was motor neurone disease and that the problem was my ribs. An X-ray revealed that my ribs were bruised, but nothing was broken.

The penny began to drop slowly for me – I couldn't keep going the way I was – and gradually I began to use the wheelchair more. I didn't want to fall again because it is a terrifying experience.

When you are in a wheelchair and being pushed by someone else, you can find yourself left high and dry –

the person pushing will say, 'I'll be back in a few minutes,' but it never is a few, and in the meantime you could end up looking at a wall and asking, 'Is there anyone here …?' That's why I chose an electronic model.

Orla Hardiman was never a fan of this wheelchair. She said it wasn't sturdy or supportive enough. In fact, it led to what Ryan Tubridy on *The Late Late Show* in November christened 'Chairgate', where Orla disagreed from a medical perspective with my choice but I insisted, because the chair allowed me to keep my independence a little longer.

Many healthcare professionals told me I would damage my back in this chair, and proposed other, larger chairs that, in my opinion, would impinge on my independence. None of the gloomy predictions have come true. I don't say this in any boastful way, I say it because it means so much to me that I can still get around on my own. When people see me in my wheelchair they see me before the chair. It might seem obvious to say, but the chair always contains a person. Yet in bigger chairs I feel that the person is consumed by the chair.

The last serious fall I had was in May while preparing to celebrate the graduation mass in a local secondary school. As I entered the hall, I tripped over a mat and came down, bashing my face on the ground.

A couple of parents arriving at that moment picked me up and, with the help of some teachers, brought me into a small office. It was obvious there was blood on my face and the principal advised me not to do the mass, that they could arrange a simple service on the spot. However, I am quite stubborn, and I was determined to say this mass as one of that year's class had sadly died by suicide during the year. I wanted to deliver a simple message to those young men. I wanted to tell them that life is precious but fragile, and that you need to hold on to it with both hands.

I also wanted to tell them to never compare themselves to others. You have all you need within you. It's all in your hands.

There was a very warm response to my being there, and some teachers helped me to the car as I made my way home to my brother's house. I don't regret for one minute celebrating that mass. I was just sorry my face looked such a mess! When I fall, it's like a tree falling in a forest – I literally fall straight down to the ground, as I don't have any power in my arms to break the contact.

The wheelchair was strange, though, because suddenly six-foot-one me became four-foot me! And some people would pat me on the head! I have to say, I've never liked people touching my head, and whenever I sensed that might be coming, I would try and put my wheelchair into fast forward.

One funny encounter was when an elderly lady approached me one day as I was going into my house. She looked at me and said, 'And how's the little fella?' I didn't know how to respond because I was almost looking for somebody behind me, the person she must surely be talking to!

I began to understand that the way people see you can change rapidly. Most people were very encouraging, and delighted that I was able to get around so freely. Others said they were praying for a miracle to happen. More would start crying, and walk away without saying anything. I continued to do several masses during the week and to celebrate weddings and funerals. It didn't seem to bother anyone that I was in a wheelchair; in fact, it has been my experience that people are helpful and gracious whenever I need their assistance.

Difficult Times

I understand why people, when going through difficult times, might be angry with God and might give up their faith because they wonder, 'What's the point? Nothing ever changes.' Others might say, 'We've had to bear much more than other people, so why us?' Since I received my diagnosis, I have been asked if I ever think, *Why me?* and to that I say, 'Why not me?' Why should I not bear some of the suffering that is in the world today?

But throughout my life, I have understood these feelings. Two things happened in early 1992, the second year of my priesthood, that were a great shock and loss to me. First, on 13 January my good friend Gerry, whom I met on my first day in Clonliffe College, died.

That first morning I woke early, but truthfully I had not slept much at all. I was full of fear and nerves at the choice I had made in my life and what would come next. However, when I went out into the corridor I heard one of the new arrivals in a room opposite me coughing very loudly. I thought he might be getting sick so I knocked on his door and this small, pale-faced, laughing young man said, 'I'm Gerry. Don't worry, I just have a bad chest.'

Gerry became my best friend and was to have a profound and lasting effect on me. He had studied commerce in Trinity College and so was a few years older than me. I subsequently learned that he had cystic fibrosis, and during the years of our studies he would spend many weeks in Saint Vincent's hospital. When Gerry was in Vincent's I often got the bus over and he and maybe one of the other cystic fibrosis patients would get dressed and we'd head out for fish and chips. Gerry was a very loving and dear friend whose wisdom and humour helped me greatly, especially in the early years of our seminary training. He had huge enthusiasm for life and dealt with his own illness with great hope. His faith never wavered, and perhaps I learned a lot from that.

By the time of our ordination, Gerry's illness had progressed considerably. Shortly before then, he took me out. We had lunch in town and then we sat down on a bench in the grounds of Trinity and Gerry heard my confession. He told me that when the end came, he wanted me to be there. At the time of his death, Gerry was curate in Rathgar parish. His health had declined very fast; he'd been due to have a transplant but he was too sick. Most days I spent with him in the hospital talking away and sometimes helping him have a bath. On the day he died I was in school in Ballymun and I was very distracted as I felt I needed to be with Gerry. Some of the teachers said I should go, as did the vice-principal. I went as quickly as I could to Saint Vincent's and in Gerry's room I found his mother Rita, father Michael and sister Michelle.

Gerry was very weak but when I called his name, he squeezed my hand. I told him that we were all there and he should let go. I said the Nunc Dimittis and a prayer by Simeon in Luke's gospel and also a night prayer of the church:

Now let your servant go in peace according to thy word: for my eyes have seen salvation which you have prepared before the face of all the people; a light to enlighten the gentiles and the glory of your people Israel.

After a few moments, Gerry stopped breathing. We all hugged one another and cried for a long time but then a peace came over us.

Gerry was laid out in the mortuary chapel. I went with Declan, another priest of the diocese, to see Gerry and when we did, we noticed that his nose was running as he lay in the coffin. We were shocked but we also laughed as we remembered a time years before when we all went to the cinema together. Owing to his illness, Gerry had a very loud, phlegmy cough. During the film, he let out one of these big coughs and a girl shouted, 'Hey snotty nose, shut up!' We all laughed so much that the attendant shone the torch at us and told us to be quiet. I have always found it strange, the way humour is so intertwined with loss and death.

Crowds of people came to Gerry's funeral in Rathgar parish. I said the mass and preached. I was joined by a large number of priests and the archbishop. That morning I asked Gerry to help me through the whole day. My heart broke for Rita, Michael and Michelle, but

I found enough courage to get through the ceremony. I was doing okay until we were carrying his coffin out of the church. I broke down then and barely made it to the door. I wondered what God was doing when such a young, vibrant priest was taken away. There is no rational answer except that Gerry died very peacefully with no anger or fear. He was sad to leave us but I know that he felt his life was fulfilled. He was at peace, and so that day, to honour Gerry and the way he approached his own death, rather than walk away full of anger, I walked away full of determination that I would tell as many people as I could about the true Jesus – the Jesus who had given Gerry peace and happiness in his final days.

Gerry was my best friend, and every day since I've missed his advice, his laughter and his devilment. We shared a love for the spiritual writer and monk Thomas Merton. Regularly we said Merton's prayer together:

My Lord God,
I have no idea where I am going.
I do not see the road ahead of me.
I cannot know for certain where it will end.
Nor do I really know myself,
And the fact that I think I am following your will
Does not mean that I am actually doing so.

But I believe that the desire to please you
Does in fact please you.
And I hope I have the desire in all that I am doing.
I hope that I will never do anything apart from that
desire.
And I know that if I do this you will lead me by the
right road,
Though I may know nothing about it.
Therefore, will I trust you always though
I may seem to be lost and in the shadow of death.
I will not fear, for you are ever with me,
And you will never leave me to face my perils alone.

Nationally, there were two stories during the first year of my priesthood which changed the Irish Catholic Church for ever.

One morning, my alarm clock radio went off to the news that Bishop Eamonn Casey had resigned. More information emerged during the day – that he had fathered a child many years before and also that there were some financial irregularities.

It's hard now to imagine how enormous this news was at the time. Casey was a well-known and popular bishop. The story was to have ramifications deep into the heart of the church, and began to shine a small light on the private lives of those who served as clergy. Now we may see that whole event in a different light and question the role of celibacy in the life of a priest. But then it was a huge scandal that raged on from week to week. And I remember being very shocked and surprised.

But far, far worse was to come when it was revealed that Father Brendan Smyth had abused scores of children over many years. I had never heard the word 'paedophile' until it was attributed to Brendan Smyth. He had abused the trust of families who had welcomed him into their homes. In a calculated and savage way he had taken away the dreams of children and replaced them with nightmares for years to come. The abuse was horrid and unforgiveable but so too was the way the church had sought to cover up these abuses. The church preaches forgiveness, and mostly this is right, but not in these cases where there is no remorse.

Faithful people had sought to tell the truth to various members of the clergy, but they were not believed. The gradual revelation that more priests had abused the trust placed in them sent shockwaves through the country and it caused great pain to me and many of my colleagues.

As I listened on the radio to the revelations, I could understand in some way the anger abuse survivors felt, as it brought me back to my own childhood. When I was around nine years of age, we had a teacher who I remember had long hair, and who wore shirts with long collars, and flared trousers. He wore a certain type of aftershave.

Several times, this man made me and another boy kneel at the back of the class. He would put his hand on our penises and do whatever he did. I can honestly say that I had no feeling about this at the time and remember little of the details. I just couldn't understand what this man was doing to me. I had no sense of right or wrong. I think I was just in shock.

I don't remember how long the abuse went on for, but I do know it stopped only when the other boy told his mother and she came down to the school. I don't know what transpired, but the teacher left shortly afterwards. Amazingly, my parents were never told by the school, and I never told them, or anyone in my family. I wanted to protect them – they were still grieving the loss of my brother Alan. There was no way I was going to add more trouble to their lives.

I have no doubt that the abuser looked at me and saw someone vulnerable: a young boy, from a family where a baby had just died, with parents who were not really paying attention. Because that's how it happens; that teacher definitely picked on me, and sadly that's what abusers do. They pick out the most vulnerable, and they prey on them. My mother might even have asked this man to keep an eye on me: 'His brother died, he's a bit delicate.' In those days, people trusted authority, and so often authority rewarded them with misery. Once you are abused as a child, it never leaves you. I never blamed God for the abuse I experienced, I blame the man who overpowered me.

As far as we schoolboys knew, that teacher had left the country. But in September of that year I was in Croke Park for the All-Ireland final with my father and my brother. At one stage I began to smell the familiar aftershave and when I looked back, there was that teacher, smiling at me. I was terrified. My father was beside me, but I didn't say a word to him. I felt almost dirty – there was an awful sense that it was happening again. And there is a lot of shame that goes with being abused. It overwhelms you. You almost feel it's your fault, because you let it happen. Even though I know now that that is rubbish, I can still feel it. That's why so many people who were abused won't talk about it. One reason why I'm writing this is because I totally understand the feelings of those who have been abused and who choose never to talk; who feel powerless and in some way robbed of their childhood, with their innocence and wonder stolen. Sexual abuse numbs the victim and leaves that event frozen in time.

But even now, I feel that if I talk too much about it, I'm giving more power to the abuser.

I never told anyone; I buried the abuse. And it went away. Except of course it doesn't – it comes out in other ways: for years, I never trusted adults. But the burying protected me for as long as I needed it, if that makes sense? The abuser takes away your power; the one thing you have left is to protect yourself until you are ready. The human psyche has an amazing capacity to hold things for years, and those memories came back to me only in therapy, when in later life I was training to be a psychotherapist.

Another very clear memory that stayed in my mind is from when I was in second class, at Saint Joseph's, Fairview. We had a teacher who was probably six feet two, and in our minds and to our tiny selves he was a giant. If anyone was bold, he would hit them on the hands with a thick piece of leather. I heard the head brother of our school often refer to the leather as 'the Minister for Education'.

One day a boy in my class got four slaps of the leather from the teacher. I could hear the boy sobbing for ages afterwards, and as we broke to go home I took the leather. I hid it and then carried it out of school with me.

Every Tuesday, my mother used to bring us into town to meet her sisters. As we crossed O'Connell Bridge, I threw the leather into the Liffey. The next day at school, the teacher called a boy up who was to receive two slaps of the leather. He opened the drawer and there was no leather. He looked at us over his glasses and said, 'Who took my leather?' I could feel my face going red, but I hadn't told anyone what I'd done, so in another way I felt very safe.

The teacher told us that he would keep us all back after school until someone owned up, but I knew that he couldn't do this because our parents would be outside. The moment passed, and by the end of the week the teacher had a new leather. But even so, my exploit filled me with satisfaction.

I often think back on the abuse and wonder where was the little boy who was able to manage? The little boy who took the leather from a violent teacher and threw it into the river. And then I think, what could my little hands do against the power of this man, the abuser? I suppose I did manage in the end – I decided to keep it to myself, to bury it deep within my consciousness where it would remain for over forty years.

The abuse revelations in the church eventually led to the publication of the Ferns Report and then the Murphy Report. Behind the wording of those reports lay the lives of hundreds of children who are now adults carrying around the scars of their abuse. They needed to know that they had done nothing wrong. That they had never invited this pain into their lives. That others used power in a negative way to take away their innocence. All the blame is attributed to the abuser and none to those who were abused. Right across the church and in society, people were knocked off pedestals that they should never have been on in the first place.

The church was humbled, and will never really recover unless it learns the true message of this humility and begins to listen to what the people of God say, rather than to the clerical few.

I will never forget the day, years later, in 2010 after the publication of the Murphy Report when I, together with so many other priests, delivered at Sunday mass the papal letter of apology to the victims of clerical sexual abuse. I was absolutely shaking. I knew the right thing to do – I had to read that letter – but I was so angry at the men who did those things to children, that I couldn't believe it. As I read out the letter, there was a silence in the church that was deafening. When I was done and my legs stopped shaking, I had to take a very deep breath. The same apology was read in every church in the country that day.

During the first year of my priesthood, 1991/92, I remember one day buying a newspaper in a garage on the Ballymun Road. Unlike other days, I was wearing my clerical collar. As I entered the shop I heard the man serving behind the counter say, 'All those priests are f**kin' perverts.' When he saw me – whom he had spoken to many times before – he said, 'I didn't mean you.' But I left feeling downcast and empty, and I knew that this was what many people felt. People were rightly angry, and so was I.

Something shifted among the staff in the school where I taught as well. It seemed like these revelations unlocked years of pent-up anger against the church over many issues. These feelings flowed down and, even though they were not directed at me, it was hard not to feel the anger and frustration.

So in many ways it had been a very shaky start to my life as a priest. At times I felt I was on a sinking ship and I know some of my colleagues felt like jumping off.

Reading back over what I have just written, it's hard, even now, to move on to talk about something else. But my priesthood is always lived through my own humanity and I am lucky that the people I served judged by what they saw and heard in me, even though they were hurt by what many in the church had done.

The Joy of Friendship

But along with the moments of darkness during that first year there were many periods of fulfilment and happiness where I knew that the choice I had made was the right one. After being placed in Ballymun, I was very happy. I had asked to be sent to a school as I felt I could communicate well with young people and I loved that aspect of my life. But it turned out that one of the best parts of the whole placement was barely mentioned in the appointment letter. I was to be stationed at Saint Pappin's presbytery which was situated beside the old church – now closed, where my mother used to go as a child – and surrounded by other houses and the famous Ballymun flats. It was laid out in such a way that I would have my own bedroom and sitting room, while I shared the bathroom and the kitchen with two other priests, Richard and Dennis.

The life of a priest can be lonely and I was very lucky to be living with Dennis and Richard at this time. Most nights, the three of us would be in my room or one of theirs watching *Newsnight* and then chatting about our day. We would have a glass of wine, and Richard and I would puff away at a cigar in my room – Dennis hated smoking. We'd often stay up talking until 2 a.m. I've been asked if it was like *Father Ted*, and my answer is always that we had more fun!

Richard and Dennis were very welcoming, and we each took turns cooking an evening meal during the week. We enjoyed each other's company. We didn't much enjoy the company of the rats, however, who were eating their way through the skirting boards into the rooms.

I remember one day I was looking out my sitting room window, which was upstairs. I was on the phone and watched while a little boy emptied rubbish into our garden. Shortly afterwards, the hall doorbell rang. I opened the door and the little boy said to me, 'Father, will you give me two pounds to pick up all the rubbish in your garden?'

I said, 'Okay.' I got him a large refuse sack and when he returned with the bag full of rubbish I said to him, 'I'll give you one pound because you used your brain and you're very clever, but I'm not giving you the other pound because I saw you throwing the rubbish in the garden yourself.'

He didn't even blush! He took the pound and said, 'Thank you, Father.'

On another occasion, we had bought paint for the house, and we left it in the garage. There were two small boys, brothers, who used to call at the door for a biscuit. One day, they called over and the younger brother said, 'We painted our house with the paint from your garage, Father!' His older brother told him to shut up.

I said, 'I hope you didn't take our paint,' and they both ran from the door at that. When Dennis came in, we checked the garage and sure enough, the paint was gone. Dennis went around to the boys' house and talked to their father and, even though the smell of fresh paint was stifling, the man denied that he had used our paint and said that we shouldn't accuse his sons. We laughed about it later, especially about the younger brother being so honest. Sometimes, honesty is not the best policy!

I loved these times and my colleagues' company and I always felt safe in that house. The only problem was: who would clean the bathroom? Within a year, however, things began to change. Richard was given a new appointment as chaplain to Trinity College, so he left. I missed him; Richard was the one who slowed down the pace of life in the house. Myself and Dennis were very alike – always on the go, organising events and meeting people. So when Richard left I could feel that some of the spirit of the house went with him, and I know that Dennis noticed it too. Within another year and a half, Dennis decided the priesthood wasn't for him and left, and eventually I moved to a small house on the Ballymun Road opposite the library. Suddenly I was living alone, and even though it gave me a lot of freedom, I did miss the company.

In UCD I lived on campus in a building called Saint Stephen's with three fellow Catholic chaplains, Kieran, John and David. I had known David for many years because we had entered the seminary together in 1985 and it was great to be in a house with other people again. I enjoy the company of others, the chance to exchange ideas and talk over any problems that might arise in the day.

I always believed that I could do something good for people, and that comes from my own childhood when I knew what it was like to be the outsider or the forgotten or the poor, in a way. Maybe because of Alan's death, and my parents' separation, I understood what it felt like to be an outsider. After my father left we had very little money so I knew what it was like to be poor. I watched as my mother was left out of the social activities around her, and through her isolation I had a sense of what it was like to be forgotten.

There is a sense of loneliness in coming home at night to a house in darkness, and cooking something to eat and thinking, *I wish there was somebody here to share this with*. But I have never regretted becoming a priest, never a day when I wished I hadn't chosen this life that I enjoy so much. I love the challenge of trying to do something, and have been let into people's lives the way no one else is. And that's an amazing privilege.

Nothing can come before Jesus Christ, but if Jesus' disciples were married, why today have we got celibate priests? Pope Francis has said that celibacy is a matter of tradition, not of doctrine. The church today is the inheritor of the ministry of Jesus and the mission of the early church. Perhaps we have lost sight of Jesus in the quest to have conformity in doctrine. I believe we must place Jesus at the centre of all we believe, and at the heart of our search for truth. I've always been fascinated by the life of Jesus and how he relates to people of all kinds. He doesn't exclude anyone, except those who place burdens on the shoulders of others. I believe Jesus met people and inspired them and accepted them as they were, and for me that will always be a blessing, in the sense that I always feel the closeness of Jesus, in every situation I've encountered.

As a priest, if I visit the sick in hospital, I believe Jesus is there for me and with me, and I simply bring that presence to the person I meet. Many in the church today have forgotten about the gospel message of Jesus and relate instead to a narrow view of church doctrine. In a way therefore they have forgotten the only commandment that Jesus gave, which is to 'love one another as I have loved you'.

Today I am administrator of two busy parishes in Dublin. The two priests who minister with me are seventy-eight and seventy-five years of age. I ask the question: who will take our places?

For myself, did the compensations of life as a priest make up for the family life I didn't have? I don't know that you can compare the two really. Nothing can compensate for a happy marriage and the joy of having children. But I would never have chosen anything else. Yes, making a life alone is a huge personal cost, but as much as I might regret that I don't have somebody here with me now who is my partner, to share this burden with me, I also think what a hardship it would be on that person.

Given the shortage of vocations all over the western world, particularly in Ireland, should we not begin to consider the idea of a married clergy working alongside anyone who still decides to choose celibacy? Again, if we look at the bible, we see the deep respect Jesus had for women, who were an integral part of his group of disciples. Most of the volunteers in our parishes are women but where are their voices heard within the leadership of the church?

Perhaps the next synod in Rome will consider these very important issues. Or at least we should discuss them within our own parishes. The local church has a powerful voice and it's time it is heard before church buildings are forced to close.

Sermon
Priesthood – Sunday, 22 May 2011

Today many people say it's a terrible time to be a priest; for some, even a waste of time. But although it has been a tough time over the past few years, I prefer to think of this as a challenging time. It is a challenge to bring the good news of

Jesus in a way that is as relevant as when he first brought it, and to help to animate and build up faith in a parish community to live the values that Jesus taught.

It will come as no surprise to hear that we have a crisis in priestly vocations today and especially in a diocese like ours with nearly two hundred parishes. We have no ordinations this year but many priests are retiring and some early because of illness. The pressure will increase on those priests already stretched in their ministry. When I entered the seminary in 1985, I was twenty-one, in a good job, and I had a girlfriend. Despite my best efforts not to respond, I was drawn to the priesthood, believing that it was what God was asking me to do, and also that God calls the weak to make them strong.

Of course 1985 was a different time and a different context from today, but what's important is that I received the support of my family and most of my friends – although some thought I was mad – and of course of the parish in which I lived. I was often sent cards of support and prayer.

I don't believe that God has stopped calling people to the priesthood. Even though, for now, women and married men cannot be priests, I know that God has put the thought of priesthood in the hearts of many. But with so much blocking that call, it can remain unheard. Also, those who might hear it may be afraid to go forward, worried about the reaction of those around them.

So if we know people who have thought about the priesthood or who we feel have the energy, optimism and will to follow Jesus, then we need to encourage them and pray for them.

To those who think of priesthood, I would offer the words of Jesus: Do not let your hearts be troubled.

Indeed, this is the clear message to each of us: Don't be afraid, and trust in Jesus. Why? Because he promised he would rise from the dead and he did. All our human striving will eventually be rewarded in heaven. So let us let go of fear and worry, and start to trust.

Vulnerability

Looking back at the early months of my diagnosis, I now see the effect the gradual decline in my health was having. At the time, however, I simply lived through it. I still had power on my right side, and my right hand and my right leg were still effective, although I quickly had no mobility at all on my left side. In fact, when I was walking, my left leg was like a heavy log dragging behind me. Because of this, I was putting huge pressure on my right side, making it do all the work. It's a strange sensation because I was not paralysed on my left side; I could still feel everything. The damage there is to the nerves, which stops the functioning of my left side but not my ability to feel sensation, good or bad.

I understood this very well when one night I came back to my house, still at that stage being renovated, to collect some post. The hall door had been double-locked and so I phoned someone who had a key. While on the call, however, the phone suddenly fell out of my hand. There are three steps up to my hall door, and as I tried to retrieve my phone, I fell onto the ground and banged my head. Unfortunately, the phone was out of reach, and I was also caught behind a skip that stood in the driveway, so I couldn't be seen from the road.

I shouted for help. Nobody heard me, so I persuaded myself to be calm and call out again. This time I was heard. A group of people rushed into the driveway, got me up from the ground and brought me into the house. I had cuts on my hands and face. A woman said her husband was a doctor and she would get him to come up. He did so, looked after the cuts, and gave me pain medication. I was in shock.

Another man who had been out for a walk with his

young daughter said he'd drive me back to my brother's house in Ballinteer in my own car. When we got there, this kind man would not accept a lift back to Mount Merrion. He said to Pat, 'You look after Tony, and we'll walk back.'

I will never forget this act of kindness.

For most of my life I have chosen to be the one who gives, or cares for others. To have that overturned with such speed was a real struggle, the sense within me that my independence was slipping away. This is the greatest battle of all – coming to terms with the knowledge that at some point I would have to let go.

I have never been good at accepting the truth of my own vulnerability but in the months since I was diagnosed, I have had to learn to let go of many of my past beliefs in order to receive help.

I remember in the early weeks and months of my illness a great feeling of vulnerability. Vulnerability is never comfortable, because everything you have learned to count on seems uncertain, but it can also summon possibilities. All my life I have been a carer of one kind or another, especially through my priesthood. At ordination I was called to be one who serves, and that is what I have been. As a carer, I shielded myself from receiving care from others. While I responded to vulnerability in others, I had yet to learn how to acknowledge my own vulnerability.

However, from early on in my diagnosis I knew people wanted to help and that this desire of theirs was genuine. There was a huge outpouring of support. In the early days, people would stop me and say, 'How are you?' and I would think to myself, 'Actually, except for MND, I'm fine.' Other people might say, 'Get well soon' or 'You've a real battle on your hands.' Actually, I have to say I don't use the words 'battle' or 'fight', because with this illness there will be only one winner. I prefer to see this as a challenge I now encounter.

I received hundreds of mass cards and letters. People were telling me that they were lighting candles in the church for me and indeed I felt the strength of this support. People also dropped a range of gifts at my door, including home-made cake, marmalade, biscuits, chocolate, flowers, and of course red wine. One of my former colleagues in UCD regularly brings home-cooked meals so that they can be frozen and used at different times throughout the week. This practical support has been immense. I suppose at this time too I was slightly embarrassed by all the attention and had to begin to understand that when you give, you must also be prepared to receive.

I knew too that if I started to refuse help, gradually it would stop being offered. In a way then it was an easy choice: I needed help and I had to accept it.

In the early days, this meant accepting help to carry shopping from the supermarket to my car. It meant asking someone to tie my shoelaces since this was one of the first things I discovered I couldn't do by myself. I needed to be helped in and out of my car. I alternated between the wheelchair and a walking stick. When I was walking with the stick, I moved very slowly, as the tiniest obstacle on the footpath could trip me up.

One of the best reliefs during the week was physio provided by PhysioFusion. Lorraine, the therapist, used to tell me she was a 'physioterrorist', as I screamed in pain when she tried to extend the fingers in my left hand, now totally closed in like a fist. She also worked on my legs and I felt great relief at these sessions. In some ways, the body heals itself, and by receiving regular physiotherapy I could feel more strength in my arms and legs. While not much can be done to halt the spread of this illness, anything I can do to help day by day is worth it.

It was late June 2009 when I met the archbishop and he told me he was appointing me as administrator of Mount Merrion Parish, which would mean leaving UCD. At the time, I was happy to leave – in fact I had requested a move – but I was surprised by the location of the new posting. The archbishop told me that the area was changing rapidly and that there would be many young families there in no time. This turned out to be true.

I began working in a parish for the first time since I was ordained. The routine was very different to what I experienced up until now. Also, I had not had much previous contact with primary schools but I loved visiting the classes and hearing the wonder and the questioning of young children. From the beginning, I wanted to ensure that the parish would be a place of welcome to anyone who called to the door, and to this day we have flags flying in the church carpark that simply say, 'Love, not judgement.'

I'm lucky that Mount Merrion was already a lively parish, with hundreds of volunteers. In January 2010 I was also appointed administrator of Kilmacud parish. The two parishes have been linked historically and several roads in the area are divided between one parish or the other. This meant that I was working in an area where there were four secondary and six primary schools. This was a huge responsibility for all the priests, and eventually both parish councils agreed they should employ a catechist. After interviews, Caroline Kehoe was offered the position, and ever since she has done wonderful work within the schools and with adult faith formation. She has also taught people how to meditate.

On Mondays, the parish team, made up of the priests, a parish sister and our catechist, held a meeting, at which important issues were discussed, including the rota of masses, for now we were all saying mass in both churches. To be honest, I have never liked long meetings, and now I have a brilliant excuse! I get very tired and nobody questions it.

One of the main features of both churches in the parish was, and is, the relatively high attendance at masses. I believe that, for many reasons, faith has become middle class in Dublin. This is interesting because in previous decades, and indeed over centuries, faith in Dublin was nurtured mainly by the poor, and yet in many of the poorer areas now, attendance at Sunday mass has declined greatly.

In both parishes I am surprised, and delighted, by the attendance of so many families, including teenage children. In Mount Merrion at 7.30 p.m. every Sunday there is a mass that is planned and concelebrated by young adults, and it is noticeable how many people in their twenties are in attendance.

Celebration of mass is about bringing communities

together and I feel this is possible if we as celebrants offer short sermons with a good splash of humour! We should honour parents who get up on Sunday morning and maybe go to some sporting event with their children and then bring them to the family mass. If we honour them, we should also respect them and realise the effort they make.

Gradually, people in both parishes have taken on more responsibility, and I'm very grateful to those who have taken leadership positions of finance, liturgy, and communications. I've always believed that the parish belongs to the people. Priests come and go; people stay where they live.

I have always known that Jesus has been with me, but with this illness I see it lived every single day and every moment of every day through the kindness, love and help of others. As my illness worsens and I become more and more dependent on those around me, I know I am blessed to be living in such a close-knit and loving parish and I feel the warmth of that every day. I hope that in my own priestly life I have brought that commandment to life for those I ministered to over the years.

The parishes also wanted to help on the Walk While You Can campaign. They quickly understood what lay behind it and started making plans to fundraise. This was great, as people who wanted to help now found an outlet where they could – through a combined effort – raise funds for MND and MND research.

This gave me more impetus. I had something to look forward to, and I'm always happiest when I'm organising something. The two parishes had raised over €60,000 before the walk even began – from a cake sale, sponsored walks, coffee mornings and a concert. The enthusiasm of those in the parishes was infectious and I knew from this early stage that Walk While You Can would be a success.

Dealing with Tragedy

As a priest you see the work of Jesus every day in the small and large kindnesses and acts of love from people. I see it every day as I live with this illness.

While in UCD, I saw the great work being done by the students with the charity work overseas. And I was amazed at how many of the academics showed true concern for the personal lives of the students. The Dean of Science, Ben, was one of those people. I had some dealings with a young first-year student from north-inner-city Dublin who had two children by the age of twenty. He passed all his exams except for maths, which he failed by 2 per cent. I talked to Ben and explained to him that this student needed to work for the summer and that repeating an exam would curtail that opportunity. Ben said to me, 'Do you want to go up and talk to the maths department, or shall I?'

I quickly said, 'Will you go, Ben?'

He laughed and headed off to the maths department, then came back and said, 'Yes, they're willing to pass him, based on all his other results.'

That student is now a Fellow of the Royal College of Surgeons. To me, this demonstrates that if you are willing to give someone a chance, very often they will seize the opportunity fully.

However, you also see at first hand immense suffering. We don't live in a perfect world but my faith calls me to respond to the world around me in whatever way I can, though again at times I have struggled with trying to make sense of things that happen.

My time at UCD was also a time of struggle and inner turmoil. Sadly, over a short period of time, five young people from different faculties in the university died by suicide.

My first encounter with this tragedy was when I received a phone call to tell me that a first-year student had hanged herself in her apartment and had been found by her friends. I learned that this student was from Northern Ireland.

On the day of her funeral, my colleagues Joe and Aoife and I met at Busáras in Dublin to get the early bus North to attend the funeral. We had decided that we would call to the girl's family home first. When I went into the house, the mother saw me and ran at me, asking, 'Why? Why?'

I said, 'I'm really sorry, I don't know.'

After the funeral, Joe, Aoife and I flew back to Dublin in a small propeller plane. I said to them, 'If only that girl could have talked to someone, maybe things would have been different.'

That night, I woke up with the words 'please talk' in my head, and I had an idea. I invited representatives from across the campus who worked directly with young people, including the Student Health Service, the Students' Union, the Chaplaincy, student advisors, those who worked in the Sports Department and university administrative staff, to meet. They all agreed that we needed to do something, so we launched the Please Talk campaign with the byline, 'To look for help is a sign of strength, not of weakness'. We wanted young people to know that help was available and that, with this help, whatever was bothering them could be heard and hopefully redressed.

In each of the tragic cases of suicide, I met with the families whose loved ones had died. One mother said to me that she now felt like she was just a ghost. Another mother wouldn't change a single thing in her son's bedroom, and told me she felt as though she was in prison for the rest of her life.

These were all heartbreaking encounters and I quickly discovered that words were useless, but the fact that I had travelled to be with the families was appreciated. Sometimes I left those houses feeling empty, and sometimes angry. I was angry because I felt it was such a waste of life, and frustrated because the young person never felt that they could tell anyone how troubled they were. My anger was directed towards a world that believes suicide is an answer. All these young people were connected to others in their lives – they had friends and indeed some of them were the only person that other classmates confided in. This smashed the stereotype of those who died by suicide – that they are somehow lonely or shy. It can often be those that feel the pressure to be a certain way, and who hide behind that image, who feel the desperation to escape.

The Please Talk campaign is now available in every third-level university and college throughout Ireland.

But it took a lot out of me and so in 2008 I requested to be moved from UCD. Looking back, I know that the impact of the suicides took away a lot of my energy and I felt I needed to go away for a time. I asked the archbishop if I could be granted a sabbatical. He agreed, although he was a bit surprised.

That summer I headed to Berkeley, California for the first part of my sabbatical. I loved the freedom of getting up each morning, buying *The New York Times* and, with my laptop under my arm, settling down to read in a local coffee shop on the edge of the Berkeley campus. I stayed there until just before Christmas.

I flew to Louisville, Kentucky to spend a month at the Trappist monastery of Gethsemani. This had been the home of Thomas Merton whom I admired greatly and in itself was the fulfilment of a dream. I'd always wanted to come here but in truth, I thought I never would.

Each day, I rose for first prayer at 3.15 a.m., followed by time for personal prayer and then mass at 6.15 a.m. After this, we had breakfast and then I worked with some of the monks, clearing out old barns on the monastery land. After this, I went for a long walk across the beautiful landscape. The weather was very cold and sometimes

I got lost, but I enjoyed the freedom I had away from phones, diaries and timetables.

After dinner, night prayer was at 8 p.m. and then everyone went to bed. I was always exhausted, so I had no problem sleeping. One day, one of the monks whose parents were from Ireland told me that he had a bottle of Tullamore Dew that he had bought in Ireland many years before. He told me that he had never been able to get the cork out of the bottle and asked me could I give it a try. The next day when I was having a shower, I brought the bottle into the shower with me and saw the cork rising.

That morning at the early morning prayer I stuck a note on the pew where he sat that read, 'Mission accomplished. It's outside my door. You can pick it up anytime.' He read the note and then took off his glasses and started looking for me, and when he saw me he gave me the thumbs up with a big grin on his face.

Also during that month I had the opportunity to say mass in the hermitage where Thomas Merton had lived. This was a great thrill and I thought of my friend Gerry, who had introduced me to Merton's wonderful autobiography, *The Seven Storey Mountain*.

From the US I flew to Israel to begin a three-month course on scripture at the Ecce Homo Centre situated in the Muslim corner of Old Jerusalem. There were over twenty of us religious from all over the world. From the building's rooftop there was a magnificent view over the city. Close to us we could see the glittering gold top of the Dome of the Rock, the old walls that surround the city and, in the distance, western Jerusalem. Every day we had lectures from scholars in Old and New Testament studies. Living in Jerusalem brought so much of the atmosphere of the gospel alive. What was also very evident was that Christians, Jews and Muslims worked quite well when it came to commerce and trading, though on the question of ownership of the holy sites, there was always tension, disagreement and negotiation.

Every week, Orthodox Jews marched through Jerusalem demanding that a new temple be built. There had been no temple in the city since AD 70 when it was destroyed. The temple area around the Dome of the Rock is claimed as the place where Muhammad descended, where Jesus overturned the sellers' tables, and the site of the original temple.

The atmosphere in Jerusalem is quite claustrophobic, with narrow streets and market shops lining each side. Crowds of tourists mix with locals dressed in all kinds of costume. There was also a mix of smells from the spices and warm meat displayed openly on the outside counters. When you reach Calvary, it is a bit disappointing because it is completely enclosed within a church. I know this is to protect the site but it's hard to imagine a hill outside Jerusalem in such an enclosed space.

The most dramatic feeling I had was when we reached Galilee. I enjoyed taking off my shoes and stepping into the cold water, reminding myself that it was here that Jesus called some of his first disciples, and here that he appeared to them after the resurrection. It was the most moving experience to imagine that I might be walking where Jesus had walked or standing at the place where the disciples were fishing.

One day our group went out in a small boat across the Sea of Galilee. We stopped in the middle and read Matthew 14:22–33

> Immediately Jesus made the disciples get into the boat and go on ahead of him to the other side, while he dismissed the crowd. After he had dismissed them, he went up on a mountainside by himself to pray. Later that night, he was there alone, and the boat was already a considerable distance from land, buffeted by the waves because the wind was against it.
>
> Shortly before dawn Jesus went out to them, walking on the lake. When the disciples saw him

walking on the lake, they were terrified. 'It's a ghost,' they said, and cried out in fear.

But Jesus immediately said to them, 'Take courage! It is I. Don't be afraid.'

'Lord, if it's you,' Peter replied, 'tell me to come to you on the water.'

'Come,' he said.

Then Peter got down out of the boat, walked on the water and came towards Jesus. But when he saw the wind, he was afraid and, beginning to sink, cried out, 'Lord, save me!'

Immediately Jesus reached out his hand and caught him. 'You of little faith,' he said, 'why did you doubt?'

And when they climbed into the boat, the wind died down. Then those who were in the boat worshipped him, saying, 'Truly you are the Son of God.'

I always loved Saint Peter, because he represents so many of us who believe until we are put to the test. In this passage, Peter was already walking on water and was completely safe until it dawned on him that he was walking on water, at which point he began to sink. But even with his doubt, Jesus reached out his hand and saved him.

After we read the piece, there was silence in the boat. All we could hear was the sound of water lapping against the sides. I can still close my eyes wherever I am and bring this scene back to life. There is no verifiable proof of the existence of God, but faith calls for belief, so it can be hard to believe what you can't see. As Jesus said to Thomas, 'Because you have seen me, you have believed; blessed are those who have not seen and yet have believed' (John 20:29).

I will never forget my time in Israel and the Holy Land. Near where we lived in Jerusalem there was a young Muslim shopkeeper. He had invited some of us to his home for food some weeks previously. On the day before we finished our course, I asked him if he'd ever been onto the roof of our building. He said no, and I invited him to come and see the view. I had some Irish whiskey left over from Saint Patrick's Day celebrations and I offered him some. He declined, as he didn't drink alcohol, but he suggested tea instead. And so a Catholic priest sat down with a young Muslim man from Jerusalem to drink tea and talk about life. It is a cherished moment.

Suicide has always been among the darkest experiences of my priesthood, especially when it was so often the death of a young person. I still hear cries of their parents as they shouted, 'WHY?' They can never answer that question and neither can I. Our response as Christians is first to try to lift the burden of the cross of another, and then to share our faith in the power of the cross and its victory over death and despair.

It is to Jesus then that we should always look for help and for answers to the 'Why?' questions that beset us.

But in my faith I believe that one day there will be an answer and I certainly will be at the top of the line asking, 'Why?'

Being away from home, away from my daily duties, living life at a different pace – these things helped to restore my sense of belief in what I could do. I went on sabbatical because I felt empty, spiritually and physically, and in a way the sabbatical filled me up again.

Reacquaintance

In as much as I have learned that receiving graciously is a gift to those who give, I also know that letting go of old mindsets and hurts can also bring us much healing and peace in our lives.

Before I left Ireland in 2008 I phoned my father to ask him if he'd like if I spent Christmas with him. He said he'd be delighted – this would be the first time any of us had spent Christmas with him since he left the family. By now he was living in San Antonio, Texas. I arrived there on 22 December.

My father met me at the airport and I was immediately struck by how small he looked. He was warm but formal. By the time we got to his house it was late, so I went to bed. He had given me his room, and the next morning he had breakfast ready when I got up. He told me he had invited some of his friends to a party that evening in the house.

Amazingly, he had very little alcohol in his house and most of the wine was corked. So we went to a local off-licence to buy good wine and he arranged for a caterer to bring food. My father had been working as a physiotherapist and a masseur, and many of the people at the party were clients of his.

I quickly realised that they had never heard of me. When I told them I was a priest, they were all perplexed as to why they'd never heard my father mention this. It was strange, but I immediately moved to protect my father and told them they had probably heard my name, but perhaps he never said I was a priest. It's funny how even after all those years I wouldn't let him down in front of people who were strangers to me.

On Christmas Eve we went for dinner to friends of his. I remember this because they asked me to say grace and one man at the table said, 'Don't forget to mention the military.' So my prayer was, 'God bless the food and the military. Amen.' They were obviously waiting for a longer prayer, because when I said 'Amen', most of them still had their eyes closed.

On Christmas Day my father and I went to mass in the cathedral in San Antonio and then had a microwaved lunch. In the evening we went to see *Phantom of the Opera*. I have to say, it was a weird Christmas Day. Just before I left the next day, my father said, 'Tony, I'm sorry for all the ways I hurt you.' All I could say at that time was, 'Thank you, Dad.'

Looking back, I know he was sincere about this apology; he had plenty of time to think about it. I was very grateful that he said it, and it lifted a huge burden I had been carrying for so many years. It had been a good visit, but in some ways I felt I had visited a stranger. I didn't want to feel this, but it was the way it was.

It was also interesting that my father gave me this apology as I was about to leave. I have found that important things are often said when there is little time for more discussion.

This time, there probably wasn't much more to say. Nevertheless, the apology was overwhelming, and asks the question, do most people deserve a second chance? Most people do, especially if they show a willingness to change and embrace forgiveness. So in my father's case I think yes. I was sad that I had never known him as his friends now knew him, but I was happy that he wasn't alone.

I kept in some contact with my father via Skype whenever our schedules and the time difference allowed it, but in the summer of 2013 we received news from America that he had liver cancer. My youngest brother, Pat, went over to be with him for two weeks. After that, David came from Australia, also for two weeks. I decided to go in August.

My father looked very well. He told me the cancer had gone, and he was back at work. What I remember most about that trip was that we went one day to Lyndon B. Johnson's house, and that my father bought a new car, something he hadn't done in twenty years.

In November we received a call from his friends in San Antonio to say that he had collapsed at home and the doctors detected brain cancer. Kieran, Pat and I flew over. It was a shock to see him in the hospital with a tracheotomy. It was made worse when the nurse came in and said loudly to us, 'And who are you guys?'

One of my brothers said, 'We're his sons.'

'And where do you live?' she asked. When we told her Ireland, she said, 'What are you doing there when your father is in Texas?'

My father's face fell – she had asked the very question that we as children had asked many times. She left the room and my father was very distressed.

The tracheotomy looked very uncomfortable and the cancer was also affecting his vision. We talked for a while and it was obvious he was very sick. We met his doctor, who told us that, with treatment, he could live for maybe three months, but the treatment was harsh. Without it, it could be weeks. My brothers and I talked to the doctor in the corridor outside my father's room. We agreed that we should ask my father to stop treatment as his condition would deteriorate quickly anyway. The doctor had said that even without further treatment, they would ensure that he would be comfortable at all times. I suggested to my brothers that we should talk to our father about what the doctor had said. They all said I was the best person to do it because I had experience.

They went to McDonald's for lunch while I went back into my father's room. I told him what we had talked about with the doctor, and even though he said he was shocked, he agreed that he should have no more treatment. Then he went quiet, and when a nurse came in, he asked her to put the armchair on the bed. She said, 'Pardon?' a couple of times, thinking she had misheard. In reality my father was in shock.

I stayed for a good while and he told me he had set up a bank account for us, his four sons, not long after he had left the family and gone to America. He told me where to find the account book in his office at his house. Then Kieran and Pat came back and I went outside to get some air.

Later that day, the hospital authorities told us we should be looking for hospice care for my father because they would be moving him out of the hospital soon. Thankfully he had very good insurance and after numerous phone calls, we found a place.

Unfortunately, we had to go back to Ireland before he was moved, so we said goodbye and promised we'd be back within a month to see him.

We were only back home two days when I received a phone call early in the morning from one of my father's friends, Ray, who said, 'I'm sorry, but your dad passed away an hour ago.' I quickly contacted my three brothers. We flew from Ireland, and David from Australia, and arrived in San Antonio late in the evening.

There we were, the four of us, at my father's house. This was the first time since 1985 that we would all sleep under the same roof. We looked around the house and there were so many things. We agreed that each of us would take a few items that we wanted to keep. Other than that, we arranged to rise at 6 a.m. every morning and clear out the house. We did such a good job that my suit jacket was also thrown out and I was the only one at the funeral without a full suit.

It was great being together as brothers during those few days. We laughed and argued in equal measure. The main sadness that we felt was for our father. He was so alone in America and at the end of his life, while we still had each other in Ireland. I know that my father was truly sorry for all the hurt he had caused us and that he understood that he could not change the past. We were not angry with him. In fact, we were happy that we saw him shortly before he died and that we were able to be together to celebrate his funeral.

We arrived at the funeral home to see our father for the first time since his death. All the employees stood up and sympathised with us, then showed us to a room where Dad was laid out. One of my brothers made a joke as if he was sitting on the bed talking to Dad. I told him to stop messing. Within moments, we were all arguing, the way we always did. We didn't know the staff were standing outside the door waiting for us, and when we opened the door and saw them, they looked shocked.

They gave us a list of items we might wish to have for the funeral, but we wanted the smallest, lightest casket they had as we planned to bury my father in Ennis, County Clare. We didn't want flowers, mass booklets or indeed anything else from the long list. One staff member asked us, 'Is it possible that an undertaker in Ireland would have no cell phone, email or fax machine?'

The next day we had a service in a neighbourhood Catholic church that my father attended. There were about eighty people there and afterwards we all returned to his house for a reception that was paid for by a friend of his.

That night, the four of us went out for a meal. A friend of my father's and his wife were at the same restaurant. They joined us for a drink and when they were leaving, the wife said, 'I feel sorry for you boys having lost your dad and now with the long journey you have back to Ireland. I want to give you this as a little gift from us.' She handed over four envelopes.

They said goodbye and we sat down at our table and, like children on their First Communion day, opened our envelopes to see what was inside. She had given each of us a thousand dollars! We had a lovely meal and great fun that night, and when we went to pay the bill, we discovered that the couple had already done so. It was a lovely end to what had been an emotionally and physically difficult week.

Back in Ireland, David stayed with me, and we had intended leaving Dublin at 7 a.m. for my father's funeral in Clare the following day. Between a late night and the jet lag, however, we slept it out, so we had to quickly get ready and drive as fast as was legal on the M50.

My mother was at the funeral, in the front row. She had said to us that this was a time of reconciliation. A few months before, when my brother Pat was in the US looking after Dad, Kieran, who lives with my mother, was on Skype to Pat. Now I should explain that my father is called Pat and my mother is also called Pat. Hearing that Kieran was talking to Pat, my mother went into the room, but by that stage Kieran was talking to Dad.

My father saw my mother through the screen and said, 'Thank you for your mass card and all your prayers.'

She replied, 'I'm very sorry you're so sick and I will continue to pray for you.'

That was the first time they had spoken to each other since 1981, so even though technology can be very negative in taking us away from each other, it seems it can also bring us together in totally unexpected ways. Shortly after this, I remember a sermon I gave on Mother's Day about families:

Sermon

In most families any secrets that come to light after spending a long time in the darkness can test the resolve of love, tolerance and forgiveness of the whole family. Sometimes we prefer not to say anything or even pretend that we do not know. Anything to keep the peace. Often it is the mother who keeps the peace, being some type of amazing multi-tasker. And indeed we have all known times when our parents knew what was going on but said nothing. In that sense they gave us some freedom.

We choose our friends but not our families, and yet it is within our families that we trust most and find our greatest safety net. It is very rare that our family will give up on us totally. There is a cost for such love within a family, however, but it is worth it.

Jesus in the gospel invites Nicodemus to come and live in the light. He might feel unworthy or indeed guilty, but Jesus does not give up on him. What Jesus states clearly is that it is better to live in the light. On a sunny day like today we can agree fully. But in Ireland we know about darkness and even on a practical level we are slow to put on lights at home.

Let us take the invitation of Jesus today and be a light – where it matters most, in our homes, in how we deal with our families, among our friends and where we work, study or play.

And when we sometimes get fed up with each other,
remember:

We are God's work of art, created in Christ Jesus
to live the good life as from the beginning he had
meant us to live it.

*****

We buried my father beside his own mother and father in a cemetery called Drumcliffe, just outside Ennis. It was a very cold November day but there was a shaft of brilliant sunshine breaking through the cloud. I remembered for a moment walking past this graveyard with my paternal grandfather when I was a young boy and being there for his funeral many years before. I was very fond of my grandfather; in the midst of the many disturbing events of my childhood, he was always a symbol of kindness. When I was young, he used to invite me down to stay with him in Clare and we'd go for a long walk and he would always say to me, 'Don't worry about anything; everything is going to be fine.' Also, he used to send money to my mother before the separation happened. When I stayed with him, he cooked his favourite dinner, bacon and cabbage, which I still love to this day. Every time I smell it, I think of him.

Psychotherapy

In the healing my brothers and I experienced with my father, I had started to realise the value of letting go of old wounds and mindsets, and this was also helped through my experiences with psychotherapy.

Before my father became ill, I had applied to do a course in psychotherapy. In my ministry, I had helped many people. But I had learned the hard way – through the deaths of young people by suicide or overdose, the waste of addiction to drink and drugs, the affliction of poverty – that there were limits to how I could help. I have always been fascinated by what makes each of us different, how we react differently to particular situations. I wanted to explore this further, so I enrolled on a four-year master's in integrative psychotherapy. But with my father's death and our trip to America, I let thoughts of the course slip from my mind. When I returned to the parish after his funeral I was exhausted. I was reading through the hundreds of cards and goodwill messages from parishioners when I had a phone call from Gearoid, who was working at Turning Point, a training centre for psychotherapy. Gearoid simply said, 'Are you ever going to do this course?' It was the prompt I needed and I told him that I would reapply the following week.

In September 2015 I gathered on day one with twenty-three other people. I remember being extremely nervous, and it wasn't helped when we were told that each of us must introduce ourselves, saying who we were, what we did, and what our main strength and weakness were. The group were drawn from all walks of life and were aged from mid-twenties to sixties. When my turn came to introduce myself, I became very self-conscious as I said, 'I am a priest.' Whatever people felt when I said this, there was no outward reaction. I went on to say that my strength was in being a good listener. My weakness was, and is, procrastination; despite all I get done, I am capable of procrastinating for far too long.

One requirement of the course is that each of us had to meet our own therapist weekly. In therapy I spoke for the first time about the abuse that had happened to me. I did so because therapy provides a safe environment and I had a good relationship with my therapist. From discussing the issue, I now feel that my own vulnerability has opened me to the vulnerability of others.

That course was one of the best things I ever did. Not alone did I get to know myself better and accept myself, but I met a wonderful group of people whom I count as friends. We know each other better than anyone else knows us.

Psychotherapy is, I believe, a process of building a relationship between client and therapist. In this process the therapist is not an expert and does not diagnose. He or she believes that the client has, within themselves, everything they need in order to befriend the challenges that face them. They might not have the awareness of how these difficulties affect them, but through the therapy process and the building of this relationship, they can hopefully find this awareness, which is the key to opening doors within them that can lead to endless possibility. I benefited hugely from the weekly sessions with Ger, a wonderful therapist. In this safe environment I opened up about the abuse that happened to me. Sometimes I hated going, possibly because I felt on the spot or felt I had nothing to say, but once I came to understand that it is my process and my time, I valued it more. In fact, it was something that I needed. To this day, I value that relationship, and therapy is a place where I can be truly myself and talk about my life as it is. By February 2018 when I was first diagnosed, I had been studying for my master's for three years and was nearing the end of the course, during which time we gained practical experience with clients.

During the first week of my diagnosis, I saw my therapist Ger, who told me to remember that the diagnosis is not the prognosis. I kept this as my mantra and in so doing, a window of possibility had been opened for me: *diagnosis is not prognosis.*

At our final session together, about a month later – we were graduating that April – we were all given an opportunity to talk from our own experience of the past three years.

I said that I was humbled by the trust my clients had put in me over the past year. I then spoke about my illness, at which point I broke down and cried, deep crying that came from my inner being. I blurted out that I had tried so hard to be strong for everyone else.

My classmates on either side of me put their hands on my shoulders and I felt that supported me. I could hear several people sobbing and tissues being passed from one person to another, and eventually into my hand. This was the first time and, as it happens, the last time, I cried about my condition.

It was a cathartic moment, and one of the class said that my vulnerability had allowed the others to enter my experience. It was as though the vulnerability I showed became an invitation to share some part of what I was experiencing. One of the tutors said they had run out of tissues!

After the tears, everyone hugged one another. I felt tremendous relief, but also emotional exhaustion. We went for a drink and some food, but I lasted only a short time as my energy had really sapped away. One of the class called me a taxi, and on the journey home I could hear the driver talking to me, but it was like he was miles away. At the time, I was in my own little world, knowing that I had all this support but also that I was truly the only one who could take each fumbling step.

I now know that the only way I can take this journey

is with Jesus by my side, and through the help of others.

All the experiences I have outlined above show the importance of family and friends in dealing with any illness – mental or physical. It's so important that those dealing with it never try to face it alone, because on your own you are isolated, but with others you feel the warmth of care.

It's also okay to cry. Tears are an expression of sadness in the same way that a smile is an expression of joy. For too long, men have tried so hard to be brave but even those who do not cry outwardly are crying inwardly. Vulnerability, I believe, is a sign of strength, not weakness. One of my nephews, when he heard of my diagnosis, was very upset. When he went out to play, his friends put their arms around him and supported him. Perhaps this younger generation are not so afraid to show different emotions or respond to a friend in need.

The moment I cried in therapy underlined the deep trust that I have always felt within this group, an experience that has turned out to be one of the most life-giving of my life. Several people in the class questioned the fact that I was not angry. But, truthfully, I've never felt anger about this diagnosis, only continual and daily frustration.

Many people say that the world has been abandoned

by God, but I firmly believe the promise in Matthew 28:20 that Jesus will be with us until the end of time. If you truly want to know about Jesus, read the gospels and hear what he had to say and how he truly lived what he said. Then you begin to open your eyes and your heart to people around you, and you see that what Jesus said is being lived out by many people today. I now live partly in the dark, but my faith in Jesus means that there is always light coming in. Like anyone else with serious illness, I too struggle, but I have never despaired. I constantly hear the words 'Do not be afraid', and then I'm calm.

Hitting the Road

The walk began on 10 July 2018 in Letterkenny, just five months after I had been diagnosed and four months after we had begun planning it. I had expected to walk at least some of the way, but in the lead-up to it I realised that this was becoming increasingly unlikely and so I took part in my wheelchair. That first morning, I was shocked to see a huge crowd outside the hotel we had stayed in the night before, including Michael Murphy, captain of the Donegal football team. My mother was there and other members of my family, along with people I've never met but who wanted to participate in this stage of the walk. This was to become a pattern each morning – we never knew who would turn up. We always had a core group of about ten people, but there could be many more. And there were many heroes – Paul, a parishioner from Mount Merrion, who agreed to drive a support car for the first week; the motor company that gave us a car; Paul Maguire and Naoise Maguire (not related), two teachers from Scoil San Treasa; all the hotels who hosted us for free, my seven-year-old nephew Mikey, who walked the full distance on the first day; Dean Gillespie, who helped with the traffic and produced two yellow flashing lights for each of our two support cars, at the front and the back.

We hit the road at 10 a.m. on that first day on what was to be a 28-kilometre walk. This was no mean feat for anyone who is not a seasoned walker. The thinking was that we should achieve the first 10 kilometres at a good pace, which led to gaps developing among the groups of walkers. Straight away, though, there was a wonderful atmosphere, with car horns honking as they passed along the road, some stopping to give us donations, and a great camaraderie among the walkers. People who had never met one another before shortened the journey by having great conversations along the way. I remember an amazing feeling that at last the walk had begun and was going well. I was delighted to be out on the road and in the fresh air. I felt well and happy. Orla Hardiman was concerned that the walk would take a lot out of me physically, and I just prayed that my own health would hold out.

We set off in a mist but before long the sun broke through and the countryside looked amazing. That was to be the story of the walk.

We arrived at our hotel in Ballybofey after about seven hours on the road and were met by the owners and staff, who were outside the hotel with yellow balloons to welcome us.

Inside they had tea, coffee and sandwiches for everyone. More importantly, they had large comfortable couches into which many of the walkers collapsed.

Over the next four days, we travelled from Ballybofey to Donegal Town and from there to Bundoran. One of the highlights was the beautiful scenery around Barnesmore Gap, where I contemplated the contrast between the huge solid edifice of the mountains around us, and the fast-changing nature of my own illness.

At one stage, we were privileged to stay in the home

of Eloise and Troy in Rossnowlagh. The house had marvellous views across the sea, with Croagh Patrick in the distance. We were to stay here for two nights, which meant that we could unpack our bags. Eloise and Troy were great hosts and provided a lovely time for Paul, Naoise, John and myself. Very early every morning that hardy crew went for a swim in the sea, after which a marvellous breakfast was cooked, with everyone making a contribution. I'd never seen so many men in a kitchen!

It was at this house one night that I found I couldn't get myself out of my wheelchair. I was in the bedroom, trying to get onto the bed, and suddenly I couldn't remember how to do it. I got a terrible fright and realised that in the space of a few days, my condition had worsened.

A friend of mine, Leslie Buckley, phoned me by chance the next day. He had been on the first leg of the walk and rang to suggest that I needed more care and that he would be willing to sponsor it by providing a physiotherapist. He was right, of course, and so I agreed, and in truth I was relieved.

On 14 July we reached Sligo through a heavy downpour, the first bad rain since we'd begun. After dinner that evening, Paul, who had the walk's official phone, told me that there was a lady in the hotel who wanted to meet me. This was Pamela Benson, a small, elegant lady who had been, for many years, a carer for Stephen Hawking. She spoke about the affection she had for him and her delight at being included in his funeral rites at Westminster Abbey. She had heard me on local radio and so came to the hotel to make a donation. This was just one of the many unexpected and incredible events that occurred during that month.

The following day, we had one of our shortest walks, from Sligo to Ballisodare. Because of this and because it was a Sunday, we had one of our biggest turnouts. Many parents with young children came along. The next day we headed to Tobercurry, where we were staying at the house of a Mrs Murphy. I was told that Lauren, a physiotherapist, would join us there, thanks to Leslie, and would help me for most of the rest of the walk.

At Mrs Murphy's we had a wonderful meal and were joined by the local parish priest. Lauren turned out to have a great sense of humour, despite being thrown in at the deep end.

The following morning we began one of the toughest legs of the whole journey as we headed to Knock. This was a 34-kilometre walk. It also didn't help that many had walked 27 kilometres the day before. One of my greatest memories was arriving into Charlestown. There were posters up welcoming us and one of the local priests came to push my chair. We turned a corner into the town and there at the right-hand side was a large footpath outside a pub. The path was lined with tables full of sandwiches and cake, with people weaving in and out offering tea and coffee.

One of the people there was Marge, who I had worked with many years before in Ballymun Comprehensive School. I asked her about the pub and she brought over the lady who owned it, who told me, 'It's closed down. My son tried to make a go of it, but it didn't work out.' I thought about this afterwards and the phrase 'the poignancy of loss and the joy of giving' came to mind. We had seen many small towns with premises closed down and yet here, despite their loss, the people gave us a wonderful welcome full of hospitality that I will never forget.

Farther along the journey in Kilkelly there were musicians playing on the street and bunting on the lamp-posts. The local pub gave me a hot whiskey. We arrived into Knock and Peter was the last; it looked like he was about to fall over. Only the stubbornness of his will got him to the end. I hadn't been to Knock since I was a child, and it looked wonderful on that sunny day.

Lauren fitted in well with the core group and was a wonderful help during the next few stages of the walk.

She helped me to get ready in the morning. Mind you, I have to be honest and say that on the first few mornings, I got up early and, with my walking stick, made it to the shower, so that I could be washed and dressed before she came into the room. But then I said to myself, 'This is stupid. I need Lauren's help, so get over it!' From then on, Lauren got me up every morning, got me dressed and, in her own way, micro-managed me for the rest of the day!

From Knock we headed to Claremorris. A local couple, Paul and Sarah, had organised an event called 'Dance While You Can'. They had a raffle where the first prize was a heifer and the second prize was a tractor service. If we hadn't known before that we were in the heart of Ireland, we did now.

There was a local band and most of the people dancing were women together, as is very common in Ireland. The hall in the hotel was absolutely packed and a local vet called John, who also lives with MND, sang a song with the band, and it was evident that the condition had affected his neck and shoulders. Just before the band started, a couple sat down beside me and told me that their 31-year-old son had just been diagnosed with the illness. His mother said to me, 'I'm absolutely devastated.' I knew exactly what she meant. My heart broke for them and I just said, 'If your son ever wants to talk to me, here's my number.'

As I journeyed on the rest of the walk, I heard many similar stories. Some people would literally stand at the garden gate and tell me the story of someone close to them living with MND or who had died recently. I was glad these people were able to tell somebody who could understand.

The next two days we journeyed through Tuam and then Claregalway. In Claregalway, Ciarán Whelan, who played Gaelic football for Dublin, joined on the walk with his young son. He probably pushed my chair 90 per cent of that walk. Then we went through Ardrahan, and on through Crusheen in County Clare. A pub had laid on a barbecue and local musicians played. Yet more warm hospitality, on a beautiful sunny afternoon.

On we went to Limerick. It was the wettest day we had experienced so far and, together with the mayor, we walked across the bridge and right through the city, but it was so wet that no-one realised what we were doing and consequently there was little turnout.

After Limerick we made our way to Adare. It was a Sunday, so we had a crowd of over a hundred people with us. At one stage a man called Isaac was pushing my chair. I noticed his New Zealand accent. He asked me, 'What are you doing when you get to Adare?'

I said, 'I'm going to find a pub to watch Cork and Limerick in the semi-final of the All-Ireland.' I told him hurling was the most skilful and thrilling sport in the world, to which there wasn't much reaction from Isaac.

Later I asked him, 'What brought you to Ireland?'

He said, 'Rugby.'

To which I replied, 'Are you Isaac Boss?'

He said, 'I am.'

I said, 'Why didn't you tell me your name?'

He said, 'No one gives their surname.'

'Well, you should have!' I told him. I was thinking about my comment about hurling. We ended up having a great conversation about life and all the ups and downs it brings. These conversations happened every day on the walk.

In the bar of the Dunraven Arms hotel, we watched a thrilling game and saw a young team from Limerick advance to the final of the All-Ireland. Lady Dunraven, whose sister lives in one of the parishes where I work, invited us for dinner at her house that evening. She is an amazing character and could literally talk for Ireland.

The rest of the walk would take us through County Cork, starting with Milford. As we entered that village, there were two women, Siobhan and Rena, on the side of the road singing 'Operator' by The Manhattan Transfer.

People behind me were wondering what was happening. For five years in the 1990s, I had travelled every Easter to Lourdes as part of a support group for pilgrims. Siobhan and Rena were also part of this group and that was one of our favourite songs to sing while there. This was another case of 'expect the unexpected'.

On 31 July we reached Mallow and stayed in the house of a woman called Tess. She had a lovely dinner ready for us, and then she left her house to us for the night and went to stay with her sister. Tess told me that her husband had died of MND and that he had been a priest many years before they met.

While in Mallow, a local doctor syringed one of my ears that had become very painful, and refused to take any payment. I also had a massage from a local masseuse who helped loosen up my limbs, which had become very tight. Again she would not take any payment. As if I needed it, these were further reminders of the wealth of kindness in Ireland. It's always there; it just needs to be tapped and it will overflow. I hope all these people realise that the small acts of kindness from them released huge gratitude in me.

The walk through west Cork took in the most beautiful countryside I've seen for years. We passed by large farms and deep green fields extending for miles. We were lucky that we walked many side roads where it was quiet, and that allowed us to breathe in the beauty around us. I thought about all the people who go to Europe to walk the Camino, and I wondered why we don't do something like that through rural Ireland.

The last few days happened in a whirl, and suddenly we were nearing the finish line. On the night of the 5th of August we had a beautiful dinner outside a restaurant in Union Hall. Two of our parishioners, Tom and Maureen, hosted the dinner for me and my family and some friends, and that night we stayed in their beautiful house in Glandore. The next morning, Maurice O'Brien, who was making a documentary about the journey, *Walking the Walk*, which was later shown on RTÉ, called to film me on the bridge between Union Hall and Glandore. It was a very poignant moment because this was the last day of the walk.

That day, the 6th of August, we set off in a mist from Drimoleague to Ballydehob. We walked over a mountain that in its haunting beauty saw us emerge from the mist towards the sunshine. Crowds of people joined us that day, with many more sitting on the bridge on the edge of Ballydehob. Two huge horses led us into the town as people clapped.

The reception had been organised by Leanne, who had done the psychotherapy course with me, and a large team of locals. There were about seven hundred people in the hall that day, all catered for by a massive army of volunteers.

The main purpose of the walk was to raise awareness of MND. The numbers who live with this illness are relatively small, but because of its complex nature, huge resources are needed to help even one person. I feel we achieved our aim, as now, thanks to all the publicity, more people than ever know what the illness is about. Secondly, we were fundraising, and have to date collected nearly €700,000, most of which has been given to Research Motor Neurone (RMN) and to the Irish Motor Neurone Disease Association (IMNDA). I'm delighted that some of that funding will pay for one more nurse to help the three already looking after people with MND around the country.

There were many heroes on the walk. The project was an enormous undertaking and yet, in organising it, there was only one committee meeting; all the planning was done by Joe, Aoife, Theresa and Holly at UCD .

We had a wonderful core group: as well as those already mentioned, there were Ros, Pat, Michael, Maureen, John, Lauren, Graham, Neil, Sarah, Carl, Liam, Codie, Kevin,

Patrick, Pat and Nuala. And there was also Michael and Maureen O'Brien – Michael was the only person to do the whole walk, and at seventy-two years of age, he gave a great example to younger people. He never complained (except maybe to Maureen!).

We are indebted to everyone who offered accommodation and acres of sandwiches and rivers of tea, all given with humour and genuine warmth. Also, nearly every member of the Research Motor Neurone team, led by Mark, took part in each stage of the walk. The wonderful website with all the information that was needed was designed by Johnny Blackmore.

I enjoyed every moment of the walk. I would do it again in the morning if someone asked me, but it would be more demanding as my own condition has worsened greatly. In fact my mobility quickly deteriorated during that time but it probably would have happened anyway. When I got home after the walk, I was nearly totally dependent, but I came home with no infections, no sores and no pain, contrary to what had been predicted. I treasure the memory as one of the best things I've ever done in my life, and I am grateful that the people who heard my proposal responded with such enthusiasm, to make Walk While You Can one of the biggest events of the summer of 2018.

Holding on to Faith

The speed of change has been the most difficult aspect of my illness. Within a few months, I had become totally dependent. I never reached any plateau where I could rest from its advances. Every day, I noticed some small change from the day before.

My faith has never wavered, and even now I believe more than ever that Jesus Christ is beside me. Every day I begin with a prayer: 'Lord, thank you for today, help me through the rest of it.' This prayer sustains me, even when I am totally frustrated by the challenges of my illness.Sometimes I pray, 'Lord, help my voice, and please sustain it, that I can always say public mass to the end of my life.' This is something I deeply treasure. Every Sunday when I preach, I simply communicate the message of Jesus and I always communicate this by saying 'we' and not 'you'. I believe that all of us gather there as brothers and sisters, and that this is a central message. Nobody in that church is excluded from the welcome and the love that Jesus gives. Many people have said that my diagnosis must have challenged my faith, but I tell them, 'The only thing that has really challenged me is the surprising and unexpected nature of my illness.' Yes, it took me totally by surprise. But then, God is the God of surprises, and in a way we should always expect the unexpected.

In the Old Testament, there are two people who I draw strength from because of the way they handled the unexpected nature of their life and their relationship with God. The first is Abraham, who always trusted God and whose faith never wavered. Even though he was assured that he would see the Promised Land, he never did. Yet he remained steadfast to all that God wanted him to do.

In his book *God, Where Are You?* Enzo Bianchi describes how Abraham responded:

> Abraham is always ready to begin anew from the beginning, to start out his journey without letting himself be trapped in the past or blinded by the future, which is, nevertheless, full of promise. Faithful to the present moment, he reaches out towards a land that is not a land, towards a place that is not a place. The true 'Place' … and the journey towards this 'Place' is an endless adventure.

I also believe that life is an endless adventure, full of hope and disappointment, laughter and tears, and many twists and turns. In Abraham I see someone who tried to remain true to his course in life.

Every Monday we celebrate a mass in the parish for everyone who is ill. At the end of the mass we read a prayer from Pope John XXIII that is more pertinent for me now than ever before:

> Every day I need you, Lord, but today especially,
> I need some extra strength to face whatever is to come.
> This day, more than any other day,

I need to feel you near me to strengthen my
Courage and to overcome any fear.
By myself I cannot meet the challenge of the hour.
We are frail human creatures and we need a Higher Power
    to sustain us in all that life may bring.
And so, dear Lord, hold my trembling hand.
Be with me, Lord, this day and stretch out your powerful
    arm to help me.
May your love be upon me as I place all my hope in you.
Amen.

The other person in the Old Testament from whom I draw strength is that very unfortunate character called Job. He was tested in many ways, and one time, angry with God, he cried out:

> Why is light given to a man whose way is hidden, and around whom God has built a wall? For I cry inside myself in front of my food. My cries pour out like water. What I was afraid of has come upon me. What filled me with fear has happened. I am not at rest, and I am not quiet. I have no rest, but only trouble. (Job 3:23–26)

Finally, God intervened and encouraged Job to be brave.

Now that God is no longer a distant God, the story ends with reconciliation, and Job proclaims:

> I know that my redeemer lives, and that in the end he will stand on the earth. And after my skin has been destroyed, yet in my flesh I will see God; I myself will see him with my own eyes. I, and not another. How my heart yearns within me! (Job 19:25–27)

Anyone who has faith knows that it will be tested from time to time. We might hang on to our faith by believing that nothing can assail us, but the challenge is always to find our faith in the more difficult moments. It can be easy to believe in the sunshine, but much harder in the rain.

This is not me being brave for the sake of being brave. This is what I believe, and that's why I can say that I don't believe we are heading to a future of emptiness, but rather a destination of hope.

Every day I sit in a reclining chair in my living room that belonged to a lady in the parish who died recently. Her family kindly donated it to me. What is amazing is that I used to bring communion to that lady as she sat in this very chair. I hate this illness. I'm not a hero; I'm simply someone living with a condition that has challenged me to live another way, and given me an opportunity to experience life as almost helpless, relying on the assistance of others. I have discovered that the greater my need is, the greater the depth of kindness I receive, which is a wonderful thing. It's often said that people want to help, and I feel that this is true. And because of this I can say I want for nothing.

It would be tempting now to spend all my time looking ahead, into the promise of the future that Jesus has given, but I find that I adhere to the idea of taking one day at a time. This means that God is present to me now, in how I experience life today, and not just as something far into the future.

Sermon
15th Sunday in Ordinary Time

The love of God that Jesus talks about is for everyone. Just as the sower throws the seed not knowing where it will land, so too the love of God is given for all. However, only those who recognise it and experience it, only those who listen to the word as we hear it today, will know that the love of God will persist and that no matter what I have done in my life, God will not stop loving me.

My Three Pillars

Over the last twenty-seven years of my ministry as a priest, I have consistently preached the message of Jesus. I base this on three pillars that I believe are essential in our church today:

1. Inclusivity
2. Compassion
3. Love

Inclusivity

In his ministry, Jesus met many people whom society cast out. When he met them, he never asked them what they had done; he was always interested in what he could do for them and how they would respond. In meeting people in this way, he included those with whom some of the religious authorities at the time would never have associated. His healing also brought inclusion.

In the story of the tax collector Zacchaeus (Luke 19:1–10), well known to children today, Jesus had dinner in Zacchaeus's house, even though all those around criticised him for going to the home of a sinner. Jesus ignored their hypocrisy. We hear Zacchaeus willing to give back all he has stolen from the people. Jesus never told him to do this. It was the experience of being included in the presence of Jesus that completely changed him.

If we in the church are truly Christian, followers of Jesus Christ, then we must make sure that we do not close doors to others through words of condemnation or harsh judgement. Once we close doors in such a way, those we have excluded will never open them again.

Compassion

The word compassion means having the ability to understand the suffering and misfortune of others. It means trying to see life from the position of the other. It is a very difficult thing to do, as we are often so busy with what's going on in our own lives. Again, in his ministry, Jesus showed that compassion. In the story of the woman caught in the act of adultery (John 8:1–11), Jesus recognises the distress of this woman, held in the middle of a circle of men carrying stones ready to kill her. She is alone (no mention of the man!) and terrified. Jesus takes his time and challenges all the men to look at themselves first:

> 'Teacher,' they said to Jesus, 'this woman was caught in the act of adultery. The law of Moses says to stone her. What do you say?'
>
> They were trying to trap him into saying something they could use against him, but Jesus stooped down and wrote in the dust with his finger. They kept demanding an answer, so he stood up again and said, 'All right, but let the one who has never sinned throw the first stone!' Then he stooped down again and wrote in the dust.
>
> When the accusers heard this, they slipped away one by one, beginning with the oldest, until only Jesus was left in the middle of the crowd with the woman. Then Jesus stood up again and said to the woman, 'Where are your accusers?

Didn't even one of them condemn you?'

'No, Lord,' she said.

And Jesus said, 'Neither do I. Go and sin no more.'

Once they had seen the imperfections of their own lives, these men stopped judging the woman through her imperfections. Because they were no different. Not alone does Jesus save the woman from death, he also restores her to her community. We don't know how that went, but one would hope there were enough sensitive people who had learned a lesson from Jesus. It's important too that this was an encounter between Jesus and a woman. In his own ministry, many women followed Jesus. This would have been counter-cultural in the Jewish tradition but not in the new discipleship inaugurated by Jesus.

We know too that Jesus wept when he heard of the death of his friend Lazarus. He goes immediately to console Martha and Mary, the sisters of Lazarus. These were friends of Jesus and he undoubtedly was a guest in their home several times during his earthly ministry. Not alone does he bring consolation to that situation, he brings life.

Jesus proclaimed that he came into the world not to condemn but to bring life. By being compassionate to others, we literally give them life and receive life ourselves.

I have always felt that believing in this Jesus would harm nobody but instead would give a deep example of how we should respond to others. This message is both ignored and adhered to in our world today. There are many examples of volunteers all over the world working in war-torn areas, where there is starvation and where people have been displaced and given the name 'migrant'. And of course, there are those who create war through corruption and greed, causing starvation and neglect. Again I find tremendous strength in Jesus as the consoler, the one who brings compassion and, ultimately, life.

Love

The greatest commandment given by Jesus was, 'Love your neighbour as yourself.'

There are more books, songs, poems and arguments about love than about any other word. It can never be fully captured, it must be lived. Every time a couple asked me to officiate at their wedding, I invited them for dinner at my house. The main reason was to get to know them better, but over a meal and a glass of wine I also got to know how they first met and what it was that now prompted them to get married. The stories of how they met were often very random, and highlighted for me the element of mystery and chance that is a core component of this life.

I really enjoyed listening to these couples, and the main lesson I learned was that, without communication – to be able to listen and to be heard – most relationships will fail. It is no coincidence that Jesus' first miracle took place at a wedding in the town of Cana, where he turned water into wine.

I've been asked several times at weddings to turn water into wine. I must say I tried a couple of times, but it still tasted like water!

When a couple on their wedding day promise to love each other for better or for worse, in sickness and in health, for richer or poorer, the reward for keeping these promises is always having the other, always knowing that there is one person in the world that will have your back. In all my years as a priest, if a couple in love came to me and asked me to bless that love, I would never refuse.

Canadian theologian Jean Vanier has said that the path to love is paved with cobblestones of forgiveness. Among his own disciples, Jesus had to forgive those who betrayed him, denied him, and ran away as he was dying on the cross, because they were filled with remorse. He understood that to love is also to forgive.

On the cross, as he is dying, in a moment of tenderness he offers a place in paradise to a criminal and then appeals to God in heaven, 'Father, forgive them, for they do not know what they do' (Luke 23:34). Even at his own moment of dying, Jesus seeks to liberate.

Many have asked why Jesus needed to die, but his cross and suffering mean he understands all those who are carrying their own cross today and those who are suffering. Our God, then, looks intimately at pain and suffering, and so can no longer be seen as a distant God. Jesus' death banishes that notion. In the book *The Crucified God*, the theologian Jürgen Moltmann says:

> The coming kingdom, the certainty of which the disciples found in the Easter appearances of Christ, has then, as a result of this Christ, taken the form of a cross in the alienated world. The cross is the form of the coming, redeeming kingdom, and the crucified Jesus is the incarnation of the risen Christ. In the crucified Jesus the 'end of history' is present in the midst of the relationships of history. Therefore in him can be found reconciliation in the midst of strife and hope for overcoming strife.

In my bedroom, I have a modern interpretation of the crucifixion. The background is painted in deep red and bright yellow. At the foot of the cross is Mary, the mother of Jesus, and the beloved disciple John. From the hands of Jesus pours a mixture of the red and yellow. I often place myself in that picture and present my own illness and frustration. I receive some mixture of the red, symbolising pain, and the yellow, symbolising hope.

The cross leads to the resurrection of Jesus. There can be no resurrection without the cross. I firmly believe in the promise of Jesus to his disciples as he was leaving them: 'I am going now to prepare a place for you so that where I am, you may be too' (John 14:3).

Gratitude and Acceptance

I have always believed that in this life we are not heading to an ending of nothingness, rather to a promise of hope. That place has been won for us by the life, death and resurrection of Jesus Christ. I totally understand the views of those who do not believe this. I know some people are perplexed that I am so definite, but I can honestly say that I have believed this all my life. Some of my best friends are agnostics and atheists and yet we enjoy each other's company immensely. We can be friends and disagree and thankfully not become enemies because I hold one point of view and they hold another. Rather, we respect each other. They know that I believe that when I die, Jesus will meet me and take me by the hand and lead me into the presence of mystery revealed. I don't know exactly the context of how it will happen. Are there gates? Are there people waiting there? Are there many rooms? Will I meet people I loved who have died? What do we do for the rest of eternity when we have only known one life? These questions will only be answered as Jesus gradually reveals what heaven is like.

Someone whom I respect greatly believes that when the brain stops, you're dead, and that's it. She said to me, 'If there is a heaven, will you come back and tell me?' I told her that I would come back some night and appear in her bedroom and she would get such a shock that she would have a heart attack and then she'd know all about it herself!

I have always preached the God of love, and as Saint John tells us: 'There is no fear in love, but perfect love casts out fear. For fear has to do with punishment, and the one who fears is not perfected in love' (John 4:18). If everyone could understand this, then the God that so many fear would be banished for ever.

While studying philosophy in the seminary, I read *The Plague* by Albert Camus. Two of the central characters are Father Paneloux and Doctor Rieux. In the town there is a plague and Father Paneloux blames it on the way in which the townspeople have been living; it is a kind of divine punishment. Doctor Rieux tries in a practical way to help all those who are ill. A child dies of the plague and Paneloux says to Rieux, 'Perhaps we should love what we cannot understand,' to which Rieux replies that he has a different understanding of love and that he would refuse to love a creation in which children can be tortured.

Like him, I too do not believe in a love that seeks to torture or hurt. In my own illness, people have asked me, 'How can a God of love allow you to suffer with this illness?' I don't see God punishing me in any way. Through my illness, I have seen the love of God in the kindness and care of so many. People have come back into my life whom I have not seen for years. With them, they bring memories from the past. I heard more conversation about mortality than I had ever expected. I suppose we all live with a massive secret: one day we will all die. There are always offers to help in many practical ways. I feel loved, and perhaps this is the healing that so many people have been praying for.

I feel so much gratitude to everyone who has tried

to help. With that gratitude, I feel a genuine sense of contentment. Gradually, I have realised that material things mean nothing. I have spent time clearing out so much of what I have gathered over the years. I felt no pang of attachment or loss, but I could not do without the love of those around me.

I also have a very strong conviction within myself that, even though I would give this illness back in the morning if it could be arranged, I do accept it. For me, this is the best way to approach serious illness. If you set out thinking you can battle or fight with MND, you will always be the loser. You will waste so much energy that would be better served preserving your strength in order that you can focus with clarity on what really matters.

When I first started training for the priesthood, I always hoped that I would be happy and fulfilled. At this point in my life, I feel that both these aspirations have been realised. I have enjoyed life and I've been lucky in the many opportunities that have come my way. For me, the meaning of life means that we are only temporarily passing through this world, and that the time we have is not as important as what we do with our lives.

Our lives will never be measured in words spoken or success achieved but rather in how we have lived and how our life has affected those around us for the better.

I know I am lucky to have a faith that has sustained me in all the different moments and challenges of my life. I don't want to brandish it in the faces of those who do not believe, I simply offer it from my own life as I have experienced it. I often think of my little brother Alan who died so many years ago. I sincerely hope that as I held him shortly before he died, he will hold me when we meet again in heaven.

Journey's End

When the fundraising walk ended, in August 2018, I was happy to be going home but I also felt the anti-climax after twenty-seven days on the road. And when I got home, I realised how further disabled I had become. The renovations on my house were complete, giving me a downstairs bedroom and wet room. It was a strange feeling, knowing I would never walk up the stairs of my house again.

Suddenly, everything became more difficult. From my wheelchair, I knew I couldn't reach the kettle or open the fridge. I realised that I would need help in the house, not just now and again, but every day. I was lucky, as my brother David was spending ten days with me before heading home to Australia. This gave me time to figure out how I was going to find the care I needed.

The diocese had arranged to fund any permanent carer that I required. I first met someone from an agency who was more intent on filling in a form than finding out exactly what I would need. Then I remembered that one of our core team members on the walk, Sarah, had mentioned that she had a friend, a nurse, who might be interested in helping me. She sent me his number and I called Adam Gaine. We agreed to meet at my house, and on the appointed day a motorbike roared into my driveway.

We chatted for a good while about the walk, voluntary work and a charity cycle that he had done. Adam was already with an agency and was very busy working nights. He was also under contract. He generously offered to fill in sometimes if I could not get someone to get me up in the morning. My heart sank, though, as I realised that this would not really work out. Adam left, but I'd had a very good feeling about him. I knew we had formed a connection, so I rang Sarah and asked her to enquire of

Adam if he would be prepared to live in my house. Adam quickly got back to me and we arranged to meet again. He said he would be happy to move in. It would take time, though, as he had to fulfil his contract, but in the meantime he did begin to help me in the mornings and suddenly I felt a great relief. I felt safe.

On returning from the walk I also realised that I could never drive again. My right hand had begun to lose its power. Already both my legs had lost theirs, so I could not stand unaided.

I have gradually watched my right hand closing so that I can no longer hold a fork or spoon and I can barely open my phone, and even that takes a huge effort as I can hardly extend my arm. After many accidents wetting my trousers, I now wear a catheter. Unfortunately, this has caused many infections. I don't sleep much as I have also developed sleep apnoea, which is a lack of oxygen in the lungs and a build-up of carbon dioxide. If I do manage to sleep, I wake up gasping for air. I need eye drops to keep my eyes lubricated as my eyelids don't close fully anymore.

I had never taken a full course of antibiotics in my adult life; now, I take several types of medication every morning and evening and throughout the day if I need it. I must also be fed now, which has been one of the hardest challenges so far.

Even though I've tried to relate some of the elements of dealing with this illness, I can't fully describe everything I feel. Every day, I must be lifted by a hoist or by several people. For someone who has never really been physically touched in my life, I now have people pulling and dragging me, washing and dressing me, straightening my jumper at the back to prevent creases, because in time these can cause pressure sores between my back and my chair.

Indeed, my world has totally changed and is almost unrecognisable from the world I once lived in. Friends of mine recently returned from America with their new baby daughter. We met for coffee one day and I watched the baby's legs shoot out in involuntary kicks, the hands not yet able to hold, and how the baby needed to be fed. In a way, I saw in the baby an image of how I am physically today. But there is one major difference. I have fifty-four years' lived experience. I have learned to adapt. Some may think that by adapting, we give away our control and freedom. However, I feel that where I have adapted, I have increased my own independence, based on my own choice. Choice is one of the few capacities I still have. It is important to hold onto some element of independence, not just in terms of control but also to insist that there is still a person there, living with the illness – the same person who was there before the illness came.

I remember when I used to visit those who had dementia, the best way to truly see them was to look into their eyes. In someone's eyes, you will always get a glimpse of the person they truly are. Sometimes you will even see a glint of the young boy or young girl they once were. Doing that has always brought me beyond the physical limits, so I do not see someone defined by their illness, I see a living person.

I want people to look into my eyes and see beyond the contortion of my body. My body may look wasted and tired, but I bet there's always life in my eyes.

I realise now that I have been able to transform some of the more difficult times of my early life into a positive way of living. Those early troubles – Alan's death, my parents' separation, the abuse I experienced – could have crushed me, or made me angry and bitter, but they did not. Because I did not let them. I know this is not possible for everyone as some of the marks of early childhood stain the adult lives of so many people, but the things that happened in my early life are the reason why I am so determined today. I have always looked at situations and seen a way to accomplish what I wanted to do; therefore, my earlier life, and the sometimes sad events in it, have not had the final word. Rather, they are the means through which I have learned that I always had a choice – either to allow what others had done to me to crush me, or to decide that they would not determine how my life would be, that only I would do that.

And so, in my illness, I want to decide how I am treated, within the care I am given. I have been very lucky with Professor Hardiman and her team at Beaumont hospital. Even though there is no cure currently for this illness, they do everything they can to make sure that life is not just bearable, but liveable. As mentioned, Adam lives with me, and not just as a carer but as somebody who makes my life enjoyable and very manageable. He has great professionalism and efficiency, but he also possesses a quality that I value more than anything: he is kind.

My doctor Gary who I have known for a long number of years – first he was a volunteer in Haiti, later I officiated at his wedding to Roisin – is in touch every week and ensures that I have all the care I need at home. On Wednesdays I have a deep tissue massage in my house given to me by Stuart, a physiotherapist who has generously dedicated time to this endeavour. Codie and Caoimhe have found a swimming pool near Stewarts hospital, Dublin which has a chair that can be lowered into the water. Together with Adam, we meet there on

Saturday mornings. The staff at the centre facilitate us by widening one lane. Being in the water gives tremendous relief and allows blood to flow faster in my legs. Through a technique called 'seaweeding', Caoimhe, who is a physiotherapist, has showed us how to move the hips in the water. For me this is the most relaxing thing I do every week. All these people have enhanced my life.

I now feel that I am facing the greatest challenge of this illness as my voice begins to weaken. My voice has been so important in raising awareness of MND, and also in my role as a priest as I celebrate public mass. I love saying mass and value the warmth I feel from those who gather there.

Perhaps the greatest frustration is one-to-one conversation when I know someone doesn't understand what I have said. They simply keep repeating, 'Yes, yes' while their faces show bafflement. I prefer people to ask me what I said, even though this will involve great effort for me, and for the person listening.

Another very annoying feature of my voice weakening is people finishing my sentences. Worst of all is people talking over me when I'm trying to speak. But I fully realise the frustration of others. Sometimes I want to scream, but then remember I can't!

Not being able to communicate fully with my voice means that I have become observant, and therefore I listen to more of what is being said. I know that soon I won't have any voice and that I'll have to find a way to communicate electronically.

When that day comes I'll have to figure out how best to deal with silence, and hope I don't sink away into irrelevance. A poem from Rumi called 'Quietness' has prompted me to see beyond what my voice contains and to journey towards the 'speechless full moon':

> Inside this new love, die.
> Your way begins on the other side.
> Become the sky.
> Take an axe to the prison wall.
> Escape.
> Walk out like someone suddenly born into colour.
> Do it now.
> You are covered with thick cloud.
> Slide out the side. Die,
> and be quiet. Quietness is the surest sign
> that you have died.
> Your old life was a frantic running
> from silence.
>
> The speechless full moon
> comes out now.

In a strange way, perhaps I'm living life more fully now than I ever did.

I mean this in the sense that I used to be running from one thing to another, and constantly busy. I used to feel that life was passing by so quickly. Now I have time, where I can move at a very slow pace through the rushing day. Now I feel, most powerfully, that I have today, and that's all I have.

This means that I get up each morning and look forward to the day, not knowing what it will bring but aware that I can take in what's happening rather than the day flying over my head. I enjoy the company of the many people who visit (even when they say 'you look very tired'), and I will persist in staying with them as long as they want. I value experiences now with more relish because I truly understand that they cannot be repeated.

My brothers are also on a journey, even though it's not theirs; they are companions of mine. David in Australia keeps in regular contact, and Kieran and Pat often help me in the mornings to get out of bed, and they also cook family dinners on Sundays in my house. I know my brothers are proud of me, but like all brothers, they give praise sparingly, in case I get ahead of myself! They have always supported me and, like all siblings, we have needed each other throughout our lives. A good sense of humour expresses our love for one another.

I know they are very sad about the illness and are probably devastated by its effects, but they answer not with sympathy, which I would hate, but with practical help and the slagging that is common among brothers. Frankly, a sense of humour is essential; without it, with this illness, you could truly go mad. We have always worked together to make things happen, including after my parents' separation, our dad's death in America, and now my illness. We argue like all siblings do, now and again, but quickly get over the nonsense that caused those arguments. It is a reminder that any illness of one family member is often borne by the whole family.

I know that my illness is also being borne by loyal parishioners in Kilmacud and Mount Merrion. They have done everything in their power to ensure that I can say mass at a small table in front of the main altar in both churches. They tell me very kindly that because my speech is affected, they have to listen harder to what I say!

I have met other people living with MND and I fully realise that even though we share the same illness, we experience it very differently. My strain of the illness is moving rapidly, but that is not the case for everyone. It is my hope that research at Trinity College Dublin and elsewhere will, sooner rather than later, be able to develop medication that is more effective in treating this condition.

The five rights of medication administration are: the right patient, the right dose, the right medication, the right time, and the right route of administration.

If anyone living with MND is reading this book, please let me clarify that I don't speak for you; rather, I outline how I have encountered the illness and how I found a way to live with its dreadful restrictions. You will have found your own way of living with it; indeed, it is part of the challenge of MND that we all have to find our own way through its complexity.

My prayer every day is very simple. I just rest in the presence of God, particularly each morning when I am awake very early. Instead of being annoyed that I can't go back to sleep, I remember that this is probably my only private time of the whole day so I literally place myself into a presence in the darkness. It's at this time that I reconcile everything going on within me and around me. This is when I am at my most calm, and I hear the words of Jesus to Peter: 'Courage. It is I, do not be afraid' (Matthew 14:27).

I have celebrated many funerals over the past twenty-seven years and have always sought to find the right words to comfort the bereaved and place the one who has died within a prism of hope. All those words are tumbling around inside me now, as if to say, 'Do you feel that the same thoughts apply to yourself?'

It is time for me to literally practise what I preach. I feel now that I am aboard a fast train with only one stop. I'm not in a mad hurry to disembark. I'm like everyone else; I only know this world and this life, but I see no meaning in this life ending in a grave. When the train stops, I will step onto that platform with hope and no fear.

Afterword
by Archbishop Diarmuid Martin

Towards the end of 2017, Father Tony Coote was the energetic parish priest of two parishes and the administrator of a third. He brought renewal and enthusiasm to the parishes in which he worked. He was universally acclaimed as a 'breath of fresh air'. He was full of ideas for the future.

A different future began to emerge, however. He had fallen in his house and he became a little worried. There was no simple explanation, so he followed the advice of his doctor and underwent tests. He was naturally worried, but never did he expect a diagnosis of motor neurone disease.

Like many others, I began googling. What we read was awful. In the months that followed, the reality of his condition began to emerge more clearly. Those who had not met Tony for some time were shocked to see how his health was deteriorating.

We were all very worried. Tony, however, rather than lose heart, as most of us would, started to make plans for the future. He decided to keep going in his ministry for as long as he could. Indeed, he would take on a new ministry for which he was not trained: living with motor neurone disease, with hope and purpose. He decided to walk the length of Ireland to draw attention to what the condition involved. Those he encountered in so many towns and villages could see the physical strain he was under: but above all, he showed how he could turn personal tragedy into hope for others.

Tony has always had an abundance of determination, and motor neurone disease did not rob him of that. Rather than feeling sorry for him, Tony made us feel humbled in the face of what he could do. His determination has given a new meaning to the expression 'a breath of fresh air'. Our admiration for Tony has taken on a new dimension.

This book is about Tony's personal story, a story that will, I'm sure, change the way each of us looks at our own life.

Thank you, Tony. May the Lord continue to inspire you with courage and determination as you face the challenges of the future.

Diarmuid Martin, Archbishop of Dublin, 2019

Postscript
by the Coote family

On the sun-filled evening of 28 August 2019, our brother Tony, after an incredible battle with motor neurone disease, succumbed to his illness and passed from this life, into the next. Despite his suffering and final, near total incapacitation, Tony passed as he so wanted, in his own bed, in his own home, in the centre of the parishes he had served so faithfully for nearly a decade. He was surrounded by his family and some of his dearest friends and was fully aware of their presence and love around him.

Tony's death was a hard blow to our family. Due to his campaign to promote the cause of MND he became a public figure to some degree. As such his death and funeral became a very public affair. Attending the services around his funeral, in Kilmacud and Mount Merrion, was an incredible experience. To see so many people from different chapters of his life was overwhelming and comforting in equal measure. Our family will always be very grateful to all those who took the time to support us in our hour of need.

Before his illness incapacitated him, Tony had something very personal in mind: to write and record his life's memoir. In May of 2019 Tony's book *Live While You Can* was launched in the Church of St Thérèse in Mount Merrion to a packed congregation of supporters and friends. It was a hugely successful event for Tony and indeed his book.

Live While You Can went on to be a bestseller for many months. It wasn't long before people started contacting Tony about his book and the effect it was having on them and their lives. People were finding parallels in their own journies and finding encouragement, strength and understanding in his words. There is honesty here, and bravery in laying bare all the moments, good and not so good, of his life. It is a journey with which many people found a connection and drew strength from.

And we, his family, are constantly consoled and reassured by people we meet everywhere how Tony's story has touched and affected their lives. That was what Tony really wanted, to spread a message of hope, faith and inclusivity.

Recently we received a message from a gentleman in Tullamore, who was diagnosed with MND in July 2019. He had met Tony in Mount Merrion and followed Tony's story. He was so inspired that he launched his own fundraiser to help with support and research for MND, as many others had done and continue to do. That's the real effect of Tony and his book: a tangible and purposeful force that helps people and gives them hope and inspiration in their lives.

And for Tony, did he get what he wanted from life: 'To call himself beloved, to feel himself beloved on the earth'? Yes! And a hundred times yes! He passed without fear into the warm embrace of that love.

Now as we all face the future and continue our own journeys we can embrace with understanding and compassion Tony's wish for us all to 'Live While You Can'.

Leabharlann

Contae na Mídhe